BABE DIDRIKSON ZAHARIAS

AMERICAN WOMEN of ACHIEVEMENT

BABE DIDRIKSON ZAHARIAS

ELIZABETH A. LYNN

CHELSEA HOUSE PUBLISHERS

NEW YORK • PHILADELPHIA

CHELSEA HOUSE PUBLISHERS
EDITOR-IN-CHIEF: Nancy Toff
EXECUTIVE EDITOR: Remmel T. Nunn
MANAGING EDITOR: Karyn Gullen Browne
COPY CHIEF: Juliann Barbato
PICTURE EDITOR: Adrian G. Allen
ART DIRECTOR: Maria Epes
MANUFACTURING MANAGER: Gerald Levine

American Women of Achievement
SENIOR EDITOR: Constance Jones

Staff for BABE DIDRIKSON ZAHARIAS

TEXT EDITOR: Marian W. Taylor
COPY EDITOR: Terrance Dolan
DEPUTY COPY CHIEF: Ellen Scordato
EDITORIAL ASSISTANT: Theodore Keyes
PICTURE RESEARCHER: Lisa Kirchner
ASSISTANT ART DIRECTOR: Laurie Jewell
DESIGN: Design Oasis
ASSISTANT DESIGNER: Donna Sinisgalli
PRODUCTION COORDINATOR: Joseph Romano
COVER ILLUSTRATOR: Richard Leonard

3 5 7 9 8 6 4 2

Library of Congress Cataloging in Publication Data

Lynn, Elizabeth A.
Babe Didrikson Zaharias.

(American women of achievement)
Bibliography: p.
Includes index.
1. Zaharias, Babe Didrikson, 1911–1956. 2. Athletes—United
States—Biography. I. Title.
GV697.Z26L95   1988   796'.092'4 [B]   87-26899

ISBN 1-55546-684-2
     0-7910-0426-0 (pbk.)

91-2341

CONTENTS

AMERICAN WOMEN of ACHIEVEMENT

Abigail Adams
women's rights advocate

Jane Addams
social worker

Louisa May Alcott
author

Marian Anderson
singer

Susan B. Anthony
woman suffragist

Ethel Barrymore
actress

Clara Barton
*founder of the American
Red Cross*

Elizabeth Blackwell
physician

Nellie Bly
journalist

Margaret Bourke-White
photographer

Pearl Buck
author

Rachel Carson
biologist and author

Mary Cassatt
artist

Agnes De Mille
choreographer

Emily Dickinson
poet

Isadora Duncan
dancer

Amelia Earhart
aviator

Mary Baker Eddy
*founder of the Christian
Science church*

Betty Friedan
feminist

Althea Gibson
tennis champion

Emma Goldman
political activist

Helen Hayes
actress

Lillian Hellman
playwright

Katharine Hepburn
actress

Karen Horney
psychoanalyst

Anne Hutchinson
religious leader

Mahalia Jackson
gospel singer

Helen Keller
humanitarian

Jeane Kirkpatrick
diplomat

Emma Lazarus
poet

Clare Boothe Luce
author and diplomat

Barbara McClintock
biologist

Margaret Mead
anthropologist

Edna St. Vincent Millay
poet

Julia Morgan
architect

Grandma Moses
painter

Louise Nevelson
sculptor

Sandra Day O'Connor
Supreme Court justice

Georgia O'Keeffe
painter

Eleanor Roosevelt
diplomat and humanitarian

Wilma Rudolph
champion athlete

Florence Sabin
medical researcher

Beverly Sills
opera singer

Gertrude Stein
author

Gloria Steinem
feminist

Harriet Beecher Stowe
author and abolitionist

Mae West
entertainer

Edith Wharton
author

Phillis Wheatley
poet

Babe Didrikson Zaharias
champion athlete

CHELSEA HOUSE PUBLISHERS

"Remember the Ladies"

MATINA S. HORNER

Remember the Ladies." That is what Abigail Adams wrote to her husband John, then a delegate to the Continental Congress, as the Founding Fathers met in Philadelphia to form a new nation in March of 1776. "Be more generous and favorable to them than your ancestors. Do not put such unlimited power in the hands of the Husbands. If particular care and attention is not paid to the Ladies," Abigail Adams warned, "we are determined to foment a Rebellion, and will not hold ourselves bound by any Laws in which we have no voice, or Representation."

The words of Abigail Adams, one of the earliest American advocates of women's rights, were prophetic. Because when we have not "remembered the ladies," they have, by their words and deeds, reminded us so forcefully of the omission that we cannot fail to remember them. For the history of American women is as interesting and varied as the history of our nation as a whole. American women have played an integral part in founding, settling, and building our country. Some we remember as remarkable women who—against great odds—achieved distinction in the public arena: Anne Hutchinson, who in the 17th century became a charismatic religious leader; Phillis Wheatley, an 18th-century black slave who became a poet; Susan B. Anthony, whose name is synonymous with the 19th-century women's rights movement, and who led the struggle to enfranchise women; and, in our own century, Amelia Earhart, the first woman to cross the Atlantic Ocean by air.

7

These extraordinary women certainly merit our admiration, but other women, "common women," many of them all but forgotten, should also be recognized for their contributions to American thought and culture. Women have been community builders; they have founded schools and formed voluntary associations to help those in need; they have assumed the major responsibility for rearing children, passing on from one generation to the next the values that keep a culture alive. These and innumerable other contributions, once ignored, are now being recognized by scholars, students, and the public. It is exciting and gratifying to realize that a part of our history that was hardly acknowledged a few generations ago is now being studied and brought to light.

In recent decades, the field of women's history has grown from obscurity to a politically controversial splinter movement to academic respectability, in many cases mainstreamed into such traditional disciplines as history, economics, and psychology. Scholars of women, both female and male, have organized research centers at such prestigious institutions as Wellesley College, Stanford University, and the University of California. Other notable centers for women's studies are the Center for the American Woman and Politics at the Eagleton Institute of Politics at Rutgers University; the Henry A. Murray Research Center for the Study of Lives, at Radcliffe College; and the Women's Research and Education Institute, the research arm of the Congressional Caucus on Women's Issues. Other scholars and public figures have established archives and libraries, such as the Schlesinger Library on the History of Women in America, at Radcliffe College, and the Sophia Smith Collection, at Smith College, to collect and preserve the written and tangible legacies of women.

From the initial donation of the Women's Rights Collection in 1943, the Schlesinger Library grew to encompass vast collections documenting the manifold accomplishments of American women. Simultaneously, the women's movement in general and the academic discipline of women's studies in particular also began with a narrow definition and gradually expanded their mandate. Early causes such as woman suffrage and social reform, abolition and organized labor were joined by newer concerns such as the history of women in business and the professions and in politics and government; the study of the family; and social issues such as health policy and education.

Women, as historian Arthur M. Schlesinger, jr., once pointed out, "have constituted the most spectacular casualty of traditional history. They have made up at least half the human race, but you could never tell that by looking at the books historians write." The new breed of historians is remedying that omission. They have written books about immigrant women and about working-class women who struggled for survival in cities and about black women who met the challenges of life in rural areas. They are telling the stories of women who, despite the barriers of tradition and economics, became lawyers and doctors and public figures.

The women's studies movement has also led scholars to question traditional interpretations of their respective disciplines. For example, the study of war has traditionally been an exercise in military and political analysis, an examination of strategies planned and executed by men. But scholars of women's history have pointed out that wars have also been periods of tremendous change and even opportunity for women, because the very absence of men on the home front enabled them to expand their educational, economic, and professional activities and to assume leadership in their homes.

The early scholars of women's history showed a unique brand of courage in choosing to investigate new subjects and take new approaches to old ones. Often, like their subjects, they endured criticism and even ostracism by their academic colleagues. But their efforts have unquestionably been worthwhile, because with the publication of each new study and book another piece of the historical patchwork is sewn into place, revealing an increasingly comprehensive picture of the role of women in our rich and varied history.

Such books on groups of women are essential, but books that focus on the lives of individuals are equally indispensable. Biographies can be inspirational, offering their readers the example of people with vision who have looked outside themselves for their goals and have often struggled against great obstacles to achieve them. Marian Anderson, for instance, had to overcome racial bigotry in order to perfect her art and perform as a concert singer. Isadora Duncan defied the rules of classical dance to find true artistic freedom. Jane Addams had to break down society's notions of the proper role for women in order to create new social institutions, notably the settlement house. All of these women had to come to terms both with themselves and with the world in which they lived. Only then could they move ahead as pioneers in their chosen callings.

Biography can inspire not only by adulation but also by realism. It helps us to see not only the qualities in others that we hope to emulate, but also, perhaps, the weaknesses that made them "human." By helping us identify with the subject on a more personal level they help us to feel that we, too, can achieve such goals. We read about Eleanor Roosevelt, for instance, who occupied a unique and seemingly enviable position as the wife of the president. Yet we can sympathize with her inner dilemma: an inherently shy woman, she had to force herself to live a most public life in order to use her position to benefit others. We may not be able to imagine ourselves having the immense poetic talent of Emily Dickinson, but from her story we can understand the challenges faced by a creative woman who was expected to fulfill many family responsibilities. And though few of us will ever reach the level of athletic accomplishment displayed by Wilma Rudolph or Babe Zaharias, we can still appreciate their spirit, their overwhelming will to excel.

A biography is a multifaceted lens. It is first of all a magnification, the intimate examination of one particular life. But at the same time, it is a wide-angle lens, informing us about the world in which the subject lived. We come away from reading about one life knowing more about the social, political, and economic fabric of the time. It is for this reason, perhaps, that the great New England essayist Ralph Waldo Emerson wrote, in 1841, "There is properly no history: only biography." And it is also why biography, and particularly women's biography, will continue to fascinate writers and readers alike.

BABE DIDRIKSON
ZAHARIAS

Babe Didrikson captured instant fame as the record breaker who single-handedly won the 1932 Amateur Athletic Union (AAU) national track-and-field championship.

ONE

"The Best at Everything"

On July 16, 1932, Evanston, Illinois, was filled with sports fans. Thousands of people from all over the United States had converged on the midwestern university town. By afternoon, most of them had gathered inside Dyche Stadium to wait for the start of an exciting double event: the 1932 U.S. Olympic trials and the Amateur Athletic Union (AAU) women's track-and-field national championships.

The street in front of the arena was empty and quiet when suddenly a taxicab raced up, its brakes screeching. Even before the cab stopped, a wiry young woman in a bright yellow tracksuit shot out and dashed into the building. Mildred Ella Didrikson—better known as "Babe"—had arrived. Sports history was about to be made.

Texan Babe Didrikson, who had checked into a nearby Chicago hotel the day before, had been up most of the night with stomach pains brought on by tension. She had finally relaxed and dozed at dawn, but then she had overslept, awakened in a panic, and frantically flagged a cab. As the car sped toward Evanston, she had scrambled into her tracksuit, desperately hoping she was not too late. When she arrived at the stadium, she was relieved to hear a loudspeaker announcement: The day's events were just about to begin.

Didrikson ran into the great concrete arena, her heart pounding. At the age of 21, she was no stranger to competition; in fact, she lived for it. But this was a very special event, one whose outcome could change her life. Inside the stadium, more than 200 women athletes, dressed in their team colors, nervously awaited the opening ceremonies. As Didrikson made her way among the competitors, a few glanced at her and smiled, but most were busy exchanging whispered words of encouragement with their teammates. Didrikson had no such supportive comrades. Her team, the Golden Cyclones, was represented by only one member: herself.

The Cyclones were a group of women athletes who played on track-and-field, basketball, and softball teams sponsored by a Texas-based insurance firm, the Employers Casualty Company. For the past two years Didrikson had worked for the company and played on its teams, dazzling Cyclones coach "Colonel" Melvin Mc-Combs—and everyone else who saw her in action—with her extraordinary athletic skills.

When Didrikson had asked her coach whether the Cyclones would compete in the Evanston contests, Mc-Combs had given her a surprising answer. She repeated it in her autobiography, *This Life I've Led*: "I think if you enter enough different events, and give your regular performance," he told her, "you can do something that's never been done before. I believe we can send you up there to represent the Employers Casualty Company, and you can win the

"It was one of those days. . . . You feel you could fly," Didrikson said of her mood at the meet where she earned a spot on the 1932 U.S. Olympic team.

national championship for us all by yourself."

Now, in Evanston, Didrikson would prove that McCombs's faith in her was justified. One by one, the announcer called out the teams' names, and each team ran into the center of the stadium. At last the loudspeaker bellowed, "The Golden Cyclones, from Dallas, Texas!" A roar of recognition rose from the stands. Didrikson, the one-woman team, took a deep, calming breath. Then, breaking into a broad grin, she trotted out onto the field, waving her lean arms over her head.

As soon as Didrikson faced the crowd, her tension evaporated and she

14

felt wonderful. "It was one of those days in an athlete's life when you know you're just right," she recalled later. "You feel you could fly. You're like a feather floating in the air."

Didrikson was entered in 8 of the day's 10 events: the 80-meter hurdles; the discus, javelin, and baseball throws; the shot put; the broad jump and high jump; and the 100-yard dash. The only events in which she was not to compete were the 50-yard and 220-yard dashes. "For two and a half hours," Didrikson later recalled, "I was flying all over the place. I'd run a heat in the eighty-meter hurdles, and then I'd take one of my high jumps. Then I'd go over to the broad jump and take a turn at that. Then they'd be calling for me to throw the javelin or put the eight-pound shot."

Didrikson won six of the events. Though she had rarely handled the 8-pound shot before, she astounded the crowd with a first-place toss of 39 feet, 6 and 1/4 inches. She broke women's world records by throwing the javelin 139 feet, 3 inches; hurling a baseball 272 feet, 2 inches; and running the 80-meter hurdles in 11.9 seconds. She leapt 17 and a half feet to victory in the broad jump. Didrikson and another competitor, Jean Shiley of Philadelphia, tied for first place in the high jump, both breaking the world record with leaps of 5 feet, 3 and 3/16 inches. The one-woman team captured fourth place in the discus throw and failed to place only in the 100-yard dash.

When the point totals were tallied, Babe Didrikson won the AAU championship for the Golden Cyclones—just as McCombs had predicted—all by herself. She had racked up 30 points, almost twice as many as the second-place Illinois Women's Athletic Club,

After setting a new world record of 11.9 seconds in the first heat of the 80-meter hurdles, Didrikson (far right) won the AAU finals with a time of 12 seconds flat.

which had 22 members. And she had secured a spot for herself on the women's track-and-field team headed for the 1932 Olympics in Los Angeles.

After the day's final event, the elated Didrikson strolled around the arena grinning, playing her harmonica, and talking to sports reporters. The writers, who knew a great story when they saw one, went wild. They called her "the super athlete" and "the wonder girl."

United Press International (UPI) wire service reporter George Kirsey described her achievements at Dyche Stadium as "the most amazing series of performances ever accomplished by any individual, male or female, in track and field history."

Such statements may have been overblown, but they reflected genuine excitement. In 1932, the world suffered in the grip of the Great Depression, a

Although she had only recently started training in track-and-field events, Didrikson displayed flawless natural form at the AAU nationals.

period of widespread unemployment and poverty that had started with the stock market crash of 1929. During those years sports were tremendously popular in the United States, for they provided troubled Americans with entertainment, inspiration, and temporary escape from personal pain. Many sports fans felt that Didrikson's triumph was their own.

That day in Evanston made Babe Didrikson an instant legend. To her fellow Americans, she was living proof that not even the depression could defeat their country. To the rest of the world, she demonstrated that the United States remained a formidable nation. Yet Didrikson had only begun her spectacular, 25-year career in sports. She would go on to conquer much of women's athletics, winning more contests and breaking more records than any woman in history.

❖ ❖ ❖

Between 1901 and 1910, almost 8.8 million people emigrated to the United States, most of them from Europe. Some fled persecution, many fled starvation, but all hoped to make new lives for themselves and their families. To some of these immigrants, the Gulf Coast of east Texas, home of the booming young oil industry, seemed like a good place to settle. The state's first great oil strike, the 1901 Lucas gusher, had come in near the city of Port Arthur. Hot, humid, reeking of raw oil, and surrounded by towering derricks,

Didrikson and Jean Shiley (right) tied for first place in the high jump at the 1932 Olympic trials, breaking the old record with leaps of 5 feet, 3 and 3/16 inches.

Like almost 9 million others, Ole and Hannah Didriksen immigrated to the United States in the first years of the 20th century in search of a better life.

Port Arthur was not an inviting spot. It was, however, a place where an enterprising, hardworking person might do well.

Ole Didriksen was such a person. A seafarer and ship's carpenter from Oslo, Norway, he sailed into Port Arthur aboard an oil tanker around the turn of the century. When he returned to Norway he told his wife, Hannah, that Texas looked like a good place to live. The couple decided that Ole would go back alone and get a job. Hannah and their three children, Ole Jr., Dora, and Esther Nancy would join Ole once he had established himself. Settling in Port Arthur in 1905, Ole

found work as a carpenter and furniture refinisher. He saved his money, bought a plot of land and, three years after his arrival, sent for Hannah and the children.

The Didriksen clan soon began to grow. First came twins, Lillie and Louis, born in 1909. Next was Mildred Ella, the future "Babe," who arrived on June 26, 1911; then Arthur in 1915. (In adulthood, Babe would claim a birthdate of 1914, but most authorities agree that the earlier date is correct. She would also change the spelling of her last name to Didrikson.) As the children arrived, Ole Didriksen built a house. About the time Mildred was born, the family moved into the sturdy wooden structure; its trim, hidden cupboards and built-in cabinets resembled those found aboard sailing ships. The house's finishing touch was a flagpole.

"America was Poppa's country now," Didrikson noted in her autobiography, "and he always wanted the flag out on the Fourth of July and Armistice Day and all the other holidays." By contrast, Hannah Didriksen never fully adjusted to life in America. She never learned to speak much English and preferred to spend her days at home. As an adult, Lillie Didriksen Grimes recalled that her mother "couldn't understand lots of what went on around her. She liked her kitchen best of all.... she was always laughin' and, oh, she loved us so

The Lucas gusher of 1901 heralded the discovery of the enormously productive oil field known as Spindletop, located a few miles from Port Arthur, Texas.

much." Hannah Didriksen was not to enjoy her shipshape kitchen for long.

On August 16, 1915, just a few hours after Arthur's birth, a hurricane struck the Gulf Coast of the United States. Mountainous waves roared through the streets of Port Arthur, killing 275 people and destroying hundreds of buildings. The Didriksen house remained standing, but as the tide came up, the building flooded. Lillie, who was six at the time, later said, "The baby was born and we left that house right away. Everything was gone in the flood. Ducks, chickens, trees, beds, money, dishes, everything." Unable to save any of their belongings, she recalled, the family "just got out of town."

For the Didriksens, as for many refugees from the Port Arthur flood, "out of town" meant up the road to Beaumont, 17 miles away. Like Port Arthur, Beaumont was a bustling oil town. The sprawling Magnolia Refinery, which employed much of Beaumont's work force, dominated the landscape. The Didriksens settled on busy Doucette Avenue, down the street from "the Magnolia," as the huge oil complex was known to Beaumont residents.

In *"Whatta-Gal,"* their biography of Babe Didrikson, William Johnson and Nancy Williamson describe the neighborhood: "God only knows what dark vapors people breathed around the Magnolia Refinery in the days when Babe was growing up. Air pollution was unknown, and, thus, unfeared, but the atmosphere was probably full of poisons; as recently as the early 1960s, pollution in Beaumont was so bad that women's nylon stockings disintegrated on their legs as they walked on the city streets."

Despite the town's unwholesome atmosphere, all the Didriksen children grew up strong and healthy. If he had no great ambition for material success, Ole Didriksen firmly believed in the benefits of exercise. He built his children a wooden gym set, complete with

chinning and jumping bars and weight lifting equipment—broomsticks with flatirons tied to their ends. "He put it there for the boys," Babe Didrikson once noted, "but my sister Lillie and I would get in there and work out with it too."

It was not an easy life. Didriksen, who had trouble finding refinishing jobs, periodically went back to sea, and his wife took in laundry and worked part-time as a practical nurse. All seven children took jobs as soon as they were old enough: By the time Babe was

In 1915 a violent hurricane destroyed thousands of homes along the Gulf Coast of Texas, forcing many families—including the Didriksens—to resettle.

in the seventh grade, she had started working after school. She got her first job at a fig-packing plant for 30 cents an hour, and then found a better one at a potato-sack factory, where she sewed burlap bags for a penny apiece and usually made about 67 cents an hour.

There was work to be done at home as well. In her autobiography, Didrikson recalled the family's life: "There were plenty of chores for all of us to do. When family washday came, each of the girls had certain things to iron. My job was to iron the boys' khaki shirts and pants.... At night we all had to shine our shoes. There were . . . 28 windows in the porch to be washed every Saturday, and the grocery shopping to be done."

Cleanliness was important to Hannah Didriksen. "Momma always believed in scrubbing floors on your hands and knees," said her daughter. 'She'd tell me, 'Don't let that dirt in the corner laugh at you! Get it out!' " When her mother was not looking, Babe made floor cleaning easier by fastening

Babe Didrikson grew up in a rough part of Beaumont, Texas, near the refinery of the Magnolia Petroleum Company (now Mobil Oil Corporation).

Most of the Didriksens' neighbors made a modest living in the oil fields and refineries that flourished in the Beaumont area.

scrub brushes to her feet and skating around on the soapsuds.

The Didriksens worked hard, but they also found time to enjoy themselves. Babe saved some money she made mowing lawns to buy herself a 35-cent harmonica, which she "could play pretty good," and which was to

give her pleasure for the rest of her life. "At first I just practiced my harmonica.... on the back porch, but finally I'd go out on the front porch where the family could hear me," she recalled. "Our whole family was musical. My brothers played the drums. Two sisters played the piano, and the other played the violin. Poppa could play the violin too. Momma sang. We had a family orchestra going there on the front porch at night after dinner.... You could see the lights going off in houses all up and down the block as people ... came out on their own porches to listen."

Babe Didriksen, who would become a first-rate cook herself, enjoyed her parents' cooking. She loved the thick oatmeal, topped with butter and sugar, that her father made every morning. Another favorite dish was her mother's Norwegian meatballs.

"There'd always be some left over the next day," she recalled. "When we got home from school, we'd slice up those meatballs and anything else that was around, and make ourselves sandwiches big enough to throw Dagwood for a loss."

Babe was a hearty eater, but food usually took a backseat to fun. One night, her mother sent her down to the store to buy some ground meat for dinner, asking her to return with it as quickly as possible. Babe ran out and bought the meat, but on the way back to the house she spotted a ball game in progress. "I stopped to watch for a minute, and the next thing I knew I was in there playing myself," she reminisced. "I was only going to play a couple of minutes, but they stretched into an hour. Along came Momma down the street looking for me. I said, 'I got the meat, Momma. It's right here.'

Then I looked where I'd left it, and there was a big dog eating up the last of that meat."

Ole and Hannah Didriksen, recalled their daughter, were "sweetly strict." Good behavior was praised, but broken rules earned swift punishment. In her autobiography, Didrikson told of coming home one day with a large rip in her brand-new dress. Her mother was in pain from a recently sprained ankle. When she saw the damaged dress, recalled her daughter, "she just blew up. She started after me, trying to run on that ankle. I said, 'Momma, don't run. I'll wait for you.' She came up to me and was going to spank me. Then she looked at me and began to laugh. She said, 'I can't whip you.' "

Like most children, the Didriksens enjoyed active pastimes: running races, roller skating, swimming in the Neches River, and playing baseball. "We'd play baseball in our back yard, and sometimes the ball would go into the rose bushes," Didrikson remembered. "Momma kept telling us to keep that baseball out of her flower beds. Then one day we persuaded her to get in the game herself. She hit a ball right into the rose bushes. We never heard any more complaints from her."

In adulthood, Didrikson would credit her mother—a renowned skater and skier before leaving Norway—as the source of her own natural athletic ability. Babe's sister Lillie was also a fine athlete, and the two girls would

Because of her talent on the baseball diamond, Mildred Didriksen's friends nicknamed her "Babe" after Babe Ruth, the New York Yankees' home run king.

often race each other, Lillie sprinting and Babe hurdling the hedges that separated yards along their street. After her sister had achieved fame as an athlete, Lillie told interviewers how Babe had "liked to practice the hurdles up and down the street. She went to every house and got them to all cut down their hedges to the right size."

Beaumont's hedges had a permanent effect on Didrikson's athletic career. "You're supposed to put your leg out straight when you hurdle," she wrote later. "But a regular hurdle is just half an inch or three-quarters of an inch thick. Those hedges were about two feet across. So I had to crook my left knee—that was the leg I always took off on—or I'd scratch myself up. That style of hurdling stayed with me. When I did get to the Olympics they tried to have me change, but I wouldn't do it."

Everyone who saw Babe in action recognized her amazing athletic gifts.

Even when very young, she could run faster, throw a ball farther, and hit more home runs than any child—girl or boy—in town. A childhood friend would later write of Babe, "She was a crack shot with a rifle. . . . a fine archer, an excellent horsewoman, captain of her own rollerskate hockey team, a good water polo player, ice skater, surf boater, canoeist, skeetshooter, billiards and pool player, boxer, wrestler and polo player." According to her sister Lillie, Babe was "the best at everything," which prompted Beaumont's children to nickname her "Babe," after home-run king George Herman "Babe" Ruth, the legendary "Sultan of Swat."

Babe never had any doubts about her future plans. "Before I was even into my teens, I knew exactly what I wanted to be when I grew up," she wrote in her autobiography. "My goal was to be the greatest athlete that ever lived. I suppose I was born with the urge to get into sports."

"Babe was blessed with a body that was perfect," noted Didrikson's high-school gym teacher. Here, she shows perfect form throwing a baseball.

TWO

Champion in Training

In high school, Babe Didrikson plunged into organized sports. Recognizing her unusual abilities, Beaumont High's coaches encouraged her to play on all the women's teams—basketball, baseball, golf, swimming, tennis, and volleyball—and she did. She would have liked to kick for the football team, but the school would not allow her to compete alongside her male classmates.

Beatrice Lytle, a Beaumont High School coach who spent 50 years teaching physical education, talked about Didrikson to biographers Johnson and Williamson. "I saw possibly 12,000 young women over those years," she said. "I observed them closely and I trained a lot of them to be fine athletes. But there was never anyone in all those thousands who was anything like Babe. I never again saw the likes of her. Babe was blessed with a body that was perfect. I can still remember how her muscles *flowed* as she walked. She had a neuromuscular coordination that is very, very rare."

Along with power and superb coordination, Didrikson had a ferocious determination to excel in every physical activity she tried. She was never satisfied unless she, or her team, came in first, and this competitiveness made her something of a loner. Although she had a few friends among both male and female athletes at Beaumont High, she was not popular with either sex. "She had a temper. She wanted to excel. She wanted to show you up," recalled Raymond Alford, one of her

Didrikson (top, second from left in front row) starred on her high-school basketball team. As a member of the volleyball team (bottom), she kneels beside Coach Lytle (in dark suit).

buddies. According to a female acquaintance, "Even in her own tough neighborhood, the other girls didn't like her because she was an athlete. Her very excellence at sports made her unacceptable to other girls. She was an alien in her own land, believe me."

"She didn't give a hang about boys—we were only good for playing sports with or to whip up on," noted Alford. Classmates often told the story of how, as a five-foot, four-inch tall freshman, Didrikson knocked out a star football player with one blow to the chin. In an era when society demanded that women devote their energies to housework, child care, and their appearance, Didrikson "did not care a hang about makeup or fussy clothing. When we talked, we'd talk about athletes" said Alford.

Didrikson excelled in all sports, but in high school she was most interested in basketball. Women's basketball was a popular sport in the 1920s. High school games drew large crowds, and many corporations, especially in the Midwest and South, sponsored women's basketball teams. Didrikson wanted to play this exciting game, but in her freshman year she was rejected by the Miss Royal Purples, the Beaumont High girls' basketball team, because of her size—she was not only short, but bean-pole skinny.

Challenged, Didrikson spent all her free time dribbling and shooting. She studied the moves and techniques of the boys' team and pestered its coach for advice on her own style. In her junior year she finally joined the Miss Royal Purples, immediately becoming the team's high scorer. On the court she was a hustler, all elbows and drive; no one intimidated her. During the next year, whenever Didrikson played, the Miss Royal Purples won. The editors of *Pine Burr*, the school yearbook, wrote of her: "She never failed to star in any game.... When 'Babe' gets the ball, the scorekeeper gets his adding machine, and then he sometimes loses count."

Didrikson's basketball talent began to attract attention, first in Beaumont and soon, as her team racked up a string of victories against other high schools, around the state. Such headlines as BEAUMONT GIRL STARS IN BASKETBALL GAME, and BEAUMONT GIRL STARS AGAIN, began appearing on newspaper sports pages across Texas. Didrikson made the all-city and the all-state basketball teams. Then, in February 1930, Colonel McCombs, a retired army officer, appeared at a girls' basketball game between Beaumont High and Houston Heights High. McCombs, manager of the Employers Casualty Company's women's athletic teams, was looking for new players, and had come to watch the star of the Houston team.

But the colonel's eyes stayed on 18-year-old Didrikson, whose amazing 26 points helped bring the Miss Royal Purples to victory. After the game, Mc-

A valuable player on her high-school baseball team (above, kneeling third from left), Didrikson was one of three on the swim team (below, at right).

Combs approached the Beaumont player with a tempting offer: a job in Dallas with Employers Casualty and a spot on the company basketball team, the Golden Cyclones. The salary, $900 a year, was an excellent one for 1930, more than a skilled typist's average of $624. "The rest of us were all excited," a teammate recalled of Didrikson's good fortune. "But after the game, up in our rooms at the Rice Hotel, Babe didn't seem to be thinking about the offer. She was too busy leaning out the window trying to see how many people she could spit at and hit on the head when they walked below on the sidewalk."

That evening, McCombs drove Didrikson home to Beaumont, where he explained his offer to her surprised

30

parents. Impressed with the high salary, but dubious about allowing their daughter to leave home and school before graduation, Ole and Hannah Didriksen said they would think it over. When McCombs left, the couple debated their youngest daughter's future.

"She wanted to go in the *worst* way," recalled her sister Lillie, "but Mama.... just hated to see her baby go." Hannah Didriksen was finally persuaded by her husband, who, said Lillie, "decided that's what they all came from Norway *for*—to give the kids everything they could in America." A few days later,

Didrikson traded in her overalls for a fashionable hat and dress as she set out for Dallas to become a "big athlete" on the Employers Casualty Company team.

her last semester of high school unfinished, Didrikson left Beaumont for Dallas—the first stop in what was to be an astonishing journey.

"You never saw anybody more excited than I was that night at the railroad station in Beaumont, Texas, back in February 1930," wrote Didrikson in her autobiography. "Here I was, just a little old high school girl, wanting to be a big athlete. And now I was getting a chance." The young woman's excitement was to be expected. She had never before traveled far from home, and now she was on her way to Dallas, 275 miles away. She had always worn bib overalls and T-shirts; now she wore a hat, a dress, and shiny patent-leather shoes. In her brand-new purse, she carried all the money she owned: $3.49.

Melvin McCombs, at the wheel of a huge, yellow Cadillac, met Didrikson at the Dallas railroad station. She was astonished when he tipped the baggage handler a quarter. "Man," she recalled thinking, "I'd like to get me a job like that!" With McCombs, she drove to the Employers Casualty Company to meet the other players. Most of them worked in McCombs's department—farmers' accident and cyclone insurance—where she, too, would be employed.

"I'd never seen so many large girls—large feet, and large hands," she recalled. Determined not to look nervous, she introduced herself to her

The Golden Cyclones won dozens of trophies in a variety of sports. In this group shot Colonel McCombs stands second from left and Didrikson sixth from left.

new teammates with her usual boisterous aplomb. One of them asked her, "What position do you think you're going to play?"

"What do *you* play?" Didrikson countered.

"I'm the star forward."

"Well," responded Didrikson calmly, "that's what I want to be." In her autobiography, she added, "And that's how it worked out, too."

McCombs, in fact, did start Didrikson as forward, the most challenging and important position on a basketball team. The same evening she arrived in Dallas, she played her first game for the Golden Cyclones, against the Sun Oil Company team, the defending national champions. Familiar with Didrikson's reputation, the Sun Oil players did their best to keep "this little kid from Beaumont" from doing any shooting at all. "They started hitting me that night, and they kept it up the whole season," she wrote later. "If one guard fouled out against me, they'd send in another one." Despite her opponents' efforts, however, Didrikson alone scored more points than the entire Sun Oil team. The Golden Cyclones won, 48–18.

Like the other Cyclones, Didrikson led a hybrid existence, half office work and half professional athletics. She lived in a five-dollar-per-month room in the same neighborhood as her teammates and ate with them at the home of one of the team's assistant coaches. "We paid 15 cents for breakfast and 35 cents for dinner," recalled Didrikson. Didrikson worked as a stenographer, and after office hours trained and competed with the other women. In addition to playing basketball, they practiced baseball, tennis, swimming, and diving.

"I didn't care too much for just swimming," Didrikson said, "but I did go for that fancy diving. I won diving events in swimming meets, and I honestly think I could have qualified for the Olympic swimming team if I had concentrated on it." Didrikson's athletic versatility was a boon to her employer. Employers Casualty, like other companies that sponsored teams, received extensive publicity for its sports programs. It was, therefore, willing to pay high salaries and spend generously for equipment, uniforms, and travel. The players could take as much practice time as they needed, and they received the best coaching available.

Didrikson thrived in the sports-centered environment, repeating the stellar performance of her first night in

A strong swimmer, Didrikson loved "that fancy diving," as she called it, and considered herself Olympic material in the sport.

game after game. She kept scoring, and the Cyclones kept winning. She was, as she exulted in a letter to a friend in Beaumont, "knocking them cold." Three weeks after she arrived in Dallas, Didrikson wrote, "Well to be frank with you I am going to make All American cause I have got my mind set on that."

Two months later, the Cyclones made it to the national basketball tournament in Wichita, Kansas. They lost the championship to Sun Oil by a single point, but Didrikson scored 210 points in 5 games and was named an all-American forward.

Soon after she started playing for the Cyclones, Didrikson began to receive employment proposals from other companies. The corporate recruiters offered various inducements: more money, bonuses for games won, free medical care. At this point, however,

When McCombs took Didrikson to see her first track meet, she was immediately drawn to the hurdles, which resembled the hedges she had jumped as a child.

34

she was much too excited by winning games and by her new status as an all-American to pay much attention to such offers.

When the basketball season ended in May, McCombs took Didrikson to a track meet, an event she had never seen. When she "saw this stick lying on the ground," she recalled, she asked McCombs what it was. "It's a javelin," he said. "You throw it like a spear." Intrigued, she picked it up and threw it.

"I got a pretty good distance," she said, "but it was so heavy—it was a men's javelin—that I slapped my back with it as I threw it, and raised a welt. Four times I slapped myself on exactly the same spot." Next, she examined the hurdles. They reminded her, she said, "of all the hedge-jumping I'd done back home. I liked the looks of that event better than almost anything else."

After the meet, McCombs decided to form a women's track-and-field team for Employers Casualty. Track was an area in which Didrikson's natural talent ignited. She had demonstrated extraordinary ability in team sports, but her great strength lay in individual performance. In addition, Didrikson seemed to possess an innate understanding of track-and-field techniques: a physical intuition that allowed her to master the sport quickly and excel at it. As one of her high school coaches later remarked, "Babe was the most

teachable person I have ever known. You could explain the rudiments of a golf swing, a basketball movement, and Babe could do it."

As soon as the track-and-field team became a reality, Didrikson got to work. "I trained and trained and trained," she recalled. "I've been that way in every sport I've taken up. After dinner I'd go out in my tennis shoes and run. . . . I'd jog my legs real high, and work my arms high, to get them in shape. Of course, they were already about as hard as they could be, but I thought they had to be better."

The night before the team's first track meet, Didrikson practiced with savage energy. After spending several hours working on her broad jump and high jump, she ran 440 yards. At the finish line, she collapsed and "saw stars" for almost half an hour. When she told McCombs about it the next morning, he asked, "What are you trying to do, kill yourself?" He lectured her about overexertion, but, she said in her autobiography, "I think he admired me for working so hard."

McCombs did admire Didrikson, but he saw her flaws as well as her good points. "Never before in my life have I seen a man or woman to compare with Babe Didrikson," he told one reporter. "She has no equal. Her only fault . . . is that she unconsciously and unknowingly overtrains. Also Babe's juvenility [childishness] and nervous energy oftentimes work to her disadvantage.

In her determination to excel in track-and-field, Didrikson practiced rigorously, often working herself to the point of exhaustion.

of 1930—only a few months after she had witnessed her first track meet—she had set new *national* records in the javelin and baseball throws, and regional records in the high jump, eight-pound shot put, and long jump.

In 1931, Didrikson scored an average of 33 points per basketball game, and was once more selected as an all-American. As her triumphs multiplied, sportswriters' accounts grew increasingly effusive. In a 1931 story, the Dallas *Morning News* called her not only "the ace of the local Golden Cyclones" but "the world's outstanding all-round feminine athlete." Her fame, however, and the way she responded to it, did not make her popular among other athletes.

One teammate, quoted in *"Whatta-Gal,"* said Didrikson "had great strength. She was born to run, to jump. . . . She was good, she was fast, she could hit the basket. But. . . . she was out for Babe, honey, just Babe." Didrikson, she added, was "not a team player. . . . But she got to be famous. And that's what she wanted." Although Didrikson pretended not to care about her teammates' unfriendly attitude, it worried her. In a letter to a friend in Beaumont, she said, "These girls here are just like they were in Beaumont High School. Jealous and more so because they are. . . . trying to beat me. But they can't do it."

Didrikson's popularity was not enhanced by her behavior off the court.

She has a tendency to brood over coming events."

But Didrikson's hard work paid off. Combined with her "teachability" and her athletic genius, it made her an immediate star in her new sport. At her first meet, she competed in four events and won all of them. By the fall

Aware that many people resented her success, she retaliated by gossiping about them without restraint. She cultivated a swaggering, tough-kid image, sometimes using locker-room language. Didrikson also refused to conform to the demands of women's fashion. One sports-page article, citing her "almost complete absence of feminine frills," reported on the difficulties Didrikson once presented a male interviewer.

Assigned to find out what "private apparel" Didrikson wore, "the poor man was blushing and stuttering in evident embarrassment." Didrikson, "in her straight-to-the-point fashion," asked him if he wanted to know if she wore "girdles, brassieres, and the rest of that junk." The interviewer nodded. "The answer," she snapped, "is no. What do you think I am, a sissy?" In the same article Didrikson commented, "I know I'm not pretty, but I do try to be graceful." And, at least on the playing field, she was more graceful than any woman athlete yet seen.

The year 1932 was to be a memorable one for Didrikson. By July, her team had come in second in the national basketball championships, she had been named all-American for the third time, and her performance at the AAU Nationals in Evanston, Illinois, had made her a sports immortal.

After she won six gold medals and broke four world records on that July afternoon in Dyche Stadium, Didrik-

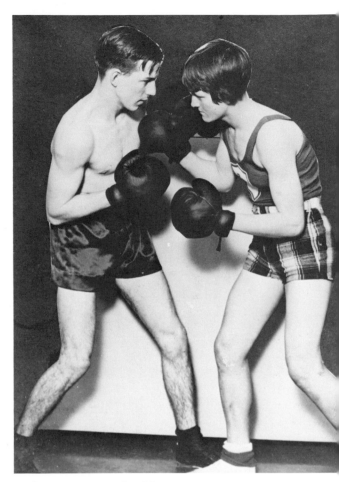

With unrestrained self-assurance, Didrikson tried her hand at almost any sport. Her aggressive confidence alienated some of her teammates.

son felt ready for the next challenge: the 1932 Olympic Games, to be held a few weeks later in Los Angeles, California. "Miss Mildred Didrikson of Dallas, Texas, who prefers to be called 'Babe,' will lead the American women's Olympic track-and-field team," reported the Associated Press (AP). "Such assistance

Didrikson (second from right) traveled to Los Angeles with the 1932 U.S. women's Olympic track team, which had elected Jean Shiley (second from left) its captain.

as she may need against the foreign invasion will be provided by 15 other young ladies."

In fact, Didrikson did not lead the team. Like the Golden Cyclones, the Olympic contestants resented what one of them referred to as her "big mouth." Didrikson did not seem to realize that her "Southern Texas talk," as she called it, alienated her quieter teammates, who considered her a braggart. The team did not want her as its captain, electing instead Jean Shiley, the Philadelphia athlete who had tied with Didrikson in breaking the world high jump record at Evanston.

Talking about her teammate years later, Shiley said, "It was impossible to get to know her because she was always chattering, talking, bragging. . . . She ran around with her medals from Evanston, saying, 'I'm the greatest, no one's better than me, Babe Didrikson.' Today people are used to flamboyant athletes. In those days athletes were supposed to be full of humility and modesty. Now we are used to people like Muhammad Ali and Jimmy Connors and Ilie Nastase."

The team traveled from Evanston to Los Angeles in a private railroad car. Hanging on its side was a huge red, white, and blue banner identifying its occupants: U.S. OLYMPIC TEAM. It was an exciting trip for the women, few of whom had done much traveling. Didrikson was especially thrilled at the thought of visiting Denver. "I was looking forward to seeing 'the Mile-High City,'" she recalled in her autobiography. "I didn't realize the slogan came from the fact that Denver is a mile above sea level. It sounds silly now, but I expected to see a city that was built a mile up in the air."

Didrikson loved Denver anyway, and if she felt disappointed at failing to make team captain, she gave no sign of it. She knew what she really wanted. As she told waiting reporters when the train pulled into Los Angeles, she was there "to beat everybody in sight."

An Olympic contender at the age of 21, Didrikson was in peak physical condition. After the games, headlines would announce, BABE BREAKS RECORDS EASIER THAN DISHES.

THREE

A Superstar Is Born

As Los Angeles geared up for the 1932 Olympic Games, a wave of excitement swept through the city. Along with almost 2,000 athletes from all over the world, tens of thousands of spectators poured into the movie capital for the games, which would prove the most spectacular the world had yet seen. Hollywood's influence permeated the atmosphere: The streets were filled with color, confusion, and glitter; promoters staged extravagant publicity stunts that gave the Olympics an air of high drama. The glamour of the movie industry and the excitement of the sports world converged that summer in Los Angeles.

To patrol the Olympic Village, where the male athletes were quartered, the film studios supplied actors dressed as cowboys and instructed to round up would-be trespassers with lassos. The biggest and brightest stars visited and posed for photographs with the Olympic contestants. Like her colleagues, Babe Didrikson was delighted with the Hollywood scene. "While I was out there," she wrote breathlessly, "I got to meet a number of the Hollywood stars I'd seen on the screen. There was Clark Gable—he could really keep you laughing. And I spent some time with Will Rogers too. He was another wonderful fellow. Then there was Janet Gaynor and Norma Shearer and Norma Talmadge and Joe E. Brown."

Meanwhile, the rest of the world looked on, enthralled by the stories printed in the newspapers each day. Didrikson and her fellow competitors

The Olympic Village in Los Angeles, the first facility of its kind, housed only male competitors; women athletes stayed in a nearby hotel.

found themselves the celebrities of the hour in a city already crowded with internationally famous stars. Reporters neglected such film royalty as Douglas Fairbanks and Mary Pickford in favor of the Olympians. Newspapers crammed their pages with details about the athletes' lives: what they ate, how long they slept each night, their favorite colors, their beauty secrets, and their advice to aspiring athletes. Sportswriters and gossip columnists vied with each other to produce the most dramatic descriptions of a city gripped by Olympic fever.

Americans, mired deep in the Great Depression, were eager for distraction and entertainment. They avidly studied every scrap of information, exag- gerated or not, about the Olympic contestants. The athletes were seen as heroes, as larger-than-life characters who would prove yet again America's strength. Didrikson stood out even from this celebrated crowd. Down- and-out Americans loved to read about the enthusiastic, confident "Texas Tornado," who would tell interviewers: "Folks say that I go about winning these athletic games because I have the cooperation thing that has to do with eye, mind and muscle.... All I know is that I can run and I can jump and I can toss things.... I just say to myself 'Well, kid, here's where you've got to win another.' And I usually do."

Didrikson and the other athletes en- joyed the publicity, but they had come to Los Angeles to work. The U.S. wom- ens' team trained regularly during the 10 days preceding the opening of the games. Didrikson prepared for 3 events: the javelin throw, the 80-meter hurdles, and the high jump. She worked out as she always had, but her hurdling style worried the coach, George Vreeland. Didrikson recalled that "I bent my front leg more than you were supposed to, on account of hav- ing practiced over those hedges back home." Vreeland suggested she straighten out her leg, but Didrikson followed Colonel McCombs's advice to stay with whatever felt natural to her and not make any last-minute changes.

On August 1, 1932, a sellout crowd of more than 100,000 people converged on the Los Angeles Coliseum for the opening ceremonies of the Tenth Olympiad. The athletes paraded into the stadium, a choir sang "The Star-Spangled Banner," and doves were released into the hot, bright air. After the Olympic flame was lighted, the athletes took the Olympic oath. The vice-president of the United States, the mayor of Los Angeles, and the chairman of the local Olympic committee made speeches while the athletes stood patiently under the merciless sun. "I couldn't enjoy the ceremonies much," commented Didrikson. "We all had to wear special dresses and stockings and white shoes. . . . I believe that was about the first time I'd ever worn a pair of stockings. . . . And as for those shoes, they were really hurting my feet." Didrikson slipped her shoes off and stood for most of the ceremony in her bare feet.

Competition started the following day, and Didrikson waited impatiently for her first event: the women's javelin throw, which did not take place until late in the afternoon. As shadows fell

Didrikson (standing third from right) and her teammates found themselves the center of attention when they arrived in Los Angeles to prepare for the Olympics.

Hollywood publicists added such theatrical elements as these cheerleaders to the Tenth Olympiad, transforming it into a thrilling spectacle.

out to make her first throw. A small German flag marked the Olympic record for the javelin toss, set by a German woman. "I was aiming to throw the javelin right over that flag," said Didrikson. And she did. The javelin hurtled straight out of her hand and took a long, low flight to set a new world record of 143 feet, 4 inches—11 feet longer than the previous record. The announcer called out the distance, and the elated athlete clasped her arms over her head, acknowledging the roar of applause.

But Didrikson's inadequate warm-up had taken its toll. As the javelin left her hand, she had felt a pop in her right shoulder. Her hand had slipped, and she had torn some cartilage. On her second and third throws, she felt sharp pains through her shoulder and realized what had happened. These attempts fell far short of her initial toss. None of her competitors, however, could match the new record she had set. She won the gold medal.

Despite her injury, Didrikson ran the heats of the 80-meter hurdle 2 days later. She ran her first heat in a world record of 11.8 seconds, easily qualifying for the finals. In the final heat the following day Didrikson ran side by side with teammate Evelyne Hall. At the starting blocks, Didrikson jumped before the gun was fired and was called back to the line. The gun sounded again, and the women took off.

and the coliseum cooled down, the women got ready for the event. Because of the crowd on the field, Didrikson could not warm up with her usual long javelin throws into the air. She decided to imitate the other competitors' technique of making short tosses toward the ground, but when she nearly injured a nearby athlete, she cut short her warm-up.

Didrikson swung her arms and stretched nervously. At last she trotted

At first, Hall led the field because Didrikson, fearful of making another false start (which would have disqualified her), held back for a split second. But Didrikson steadily gained on Hall, and caught up just two hurdles from the finish line. Both women held their pace, breaking the tape in tandem.

Throwing up her arms exuberantly, Didrikson shouted to Hall, "Well, I won again." Hall related the painful moment to interviewers: "I turned and saw some athletes in the crowd cheering me, holding up one finger to show me that I was first. I shook my head and held up two fingers to them. Later,

Didrikson usually displayed classic form in the javelin throw, but she lost her grip and injured her shoulder when making the toss that shattered the world record.

Winning the first heat of the Olympic 80-meter hurdles with a time of 11.8 seconds, Didrikson (right) broke the record she had set at the AAU nationals.

In the 80-meter hurdle finals, Didrikson (left) shot out her arm as she broke the tape alongside Evelyne Hall (right), convincing the judges that she had won.

I learned that at that very moment a couple of judges were looking at me. It's possible they made their judgment from this gesture of mine."

The timer said that both women had reached the tape in 11.7 seconds, a new world record. Films of the race showed them finishing dead even: No one could say for sure which woman— if any—actually won the race. But the judges, perhaps because Didrikson was the audience's favorite, awarded her the gold medal. The press splashed the news of her triumph across the front pages of the nation's papers, fortifying the Didrikson legend. Sports fans responded to the young woman's double victory with wild enthusiasm. Excitement built as she approached her third event, the high jump.

Babe Didrikson intended to be the first woman to win three track-and-field gold medals in a single Olympic year, and she knew she had a good chance with the high jump. She seemed unstoppable as the bar went up and, one by one, competitors dropped out. Finally, only she and Jean Shiley remained, and the bar stood at five feet, five and one-quarter inches. The competition was a face-off between the two teammates who had tied in the high jump and broken the world record at the AAU Nationals.

Both women cleared the bar, setting a new world record. The bar was raised an inch, to five feet, six and one-quarter inches. Didrikson jumped first. "I went

Tied with Shiley in the high jump, Didrikson cleared the world-record height but lost the gold medal when judges ruled her jump an illegal dive.

into my Western roll, kicking up and rolling over," she said. "I just soared up there. I felt like a bird. I could see that bar several inches beneath me as I went across. I was up around five-ten, higher than I had ever been."

As she dropped into the sandpit, however, Didrikson's foot struck one of the posts supporting the bar. The bar jarred loose and fell. The judges ruled the jump a miss. Shiley jumped and also missed. The bar dropped back down to the world record height. Both women jumped again, and again both made it over the bar. It looked like a tie, but then the judges announced that Didrikson's jump was illegal. Her Western-roll technique, unfamiliar to American officials at the time, looked too much like a dive to the Olympic judges.

Most high jumpers used a scissor jump that took them over the bar in a basically vertical position. "In the

Western roll," Didrikson explained, "you kick up there and roll over the bar flat. Under the high-jump rules they had at that time, your feet had to go over the bar first." The diving rule has since been revoked, but in 1932 Didrikson could not convince the judges her jump was legal. She protested loudly, but to no avail. Shiley took the gold medal, leaving Didrikson the silver.

The episode did not diminish Didrikson's stature in the eyes of her fans and supporters. Many sportswriters—who had seen it all from their box in the stands—stood steadfastly behind Didrikson, both privately and in print. Grantland Rice, the premier sportswriter of the period, hailed her as "the most flawless section of muscle harmony, of complete mental and physical coordination the world of sport has ever known." Thanks to praise like this, a superstar—smasher of world records, winner of three Olympic medals, public personality—was born.

Grantland Rice not only admired Didrikson on a professional level; he was her personal friend. The afternoon

When she played golf with Grantland Rice (left) after the Olympics, Didrikson recalled, "That was the day that really determined" that she would become a golfer.

Cheering fans surround Didrikson as she rides through the streets of Dallas. Pennants proclaim the native Texan OUR BABE.

of the high jump competition, he extended a fateful invitation to her: He asked her to play golf with him at a Los Angeles country club. It was not the first time that Didrikson would play the game. In fact, Beatrice Lytle, her high school gym teacher, recalled teaching Didrikson the game a few years earlier. "I showed Babe her first golf club around nineteen twenty-seven, I guess," Lytle told interviewers. "Babe took to the game quite well,

although it was all quite rudimentary."

Rice was sure Didrikson could develop into much more than a "rudimentary" golf player. When Didrikson joined him and three other sportswriters for a round of golf the day after winning her silver medal, she took her first step toward golf fame. Her superb physical condition and extraordinary strength allowed her to drive the ball incredible distances—sometimes 250 yards or more—thrilling her journalist

Didrikson's proud family joined her in Dallas for the post-Olympic celebration. From left to right are Lillie, Ole, Babe, and Hannah.

friends. Her game was rough and uneven, and she scored an unexceptional 95, but Rice and his friends reported on her golf prowess in glowing terms.

"She is the longest hitter women's golf has ever seen, for she has a free, lashing style backed up with championship form and terrific power in strong hands, strong wrists, forearms of steel," wrote the admiring Rice. From that day on, Didrikson knew she wanted to play championship golf. It would, however, be a few years before she could pursue this dream.

At the close of the Olympic Games, Didrikson returned to Texas. The Em-

ployers Casualty Company paid for her plane ticket from Los Angeles to Dallas, where the police-department band and the fire chief's red limousine awaited her arrival. Prominent Dallas citizens, officials from Employers Casualty, members of the Golden Cyclones, and crowds of fans greeted Didrikson at the airport. The athlete climbed into the backseat of the limousine, which was piled with red roses, and a parade set off through the streets of Dallas.

The Didriksen family had driven from Beaumont to help celebrate. They arrived dusty and sweaty from the long trip, in a car with two flat tires. But when she saw her sister Lillie, Babe insisted she join her in the seat of honor. "The big shots," Lillie recalled, "they was all looking at us country folks, but we didn't care. Babe didn't care. We had our parade through Dallas." A long line of cars, with the limousine at its head, drove through the city to the Adolphus Hotel, while people waved and threw confetti from the windows of buildings. The Didriksens stayed in a flower-filled suite during two days of festivities.

Didrikson bought her family new tires for their return trip, then took off for her hometown in a small, single-engine plane. It seemed that all of Beaumont turned out to greet her at the airstrip. The high school band, a Miss Royal Purples honor guard, the mayor, and various civic leaders formed a parade through the city's streets, with Didrikson riding in the fire chief's car. Beaumont's most famous citizen was lauded in speeches and given the key to the city. At the age of 21, the young woman who had grown up in the shadow of the Magnolia had become a star.

Didrikson signs a contract while her manager, George Emerson (seated), looks on. As a professional, Didrikson would play a wide variety of sports.

FOUR

The Professional

Babe Didrikson reveled in the fame she had attained at the Olympics. She granted dozens of interviews and made numerous public appearances, such as competing at a post-Olympic amateur track meet in Chicago. But she could not live on admiration—she needed an income. The Illinois Women's Athletic Club offered her the generous sum of $300 per month to join their team, but she felt torn because she did not want to leave Texas. Didrikson told Colonel McCombs of the offer, and when he matched it, she went back to work for Employers Casualty.

With her first paychecks, Didrikson bought clothing for her entire family and a new stove and icebox for her mother. She then purchased an expensive, red Dodge coupe, an acquisition that would change the course of her career. Less than a month after she bought the car, Didrikson's name and photograph appeared in a Dodge advertisement. Dodge publicity agents quoted her as saying, "Speed—unyielding strength—enduring stamina—that's the stuff that makes real champions, whether they're in the athletic arena or in the world of automobiles."

It seemed obvious that the plainspoken Didrikson had never said any such thing, but the Amateur Athletic Union promptly revoked her amateur status for advertising the car. The AAU accused her of violating regulations against accepting pay for athletics or promotional work. Suspended indefi-

Seated to the right of Colonel McCombs, an unhappy Didrikson watches the Golden Cyclones play basketball. Her suspension from the AAU barred her from the team.

nitely from amateur competition, Didrikson could no longer play for the Golden Cyclones.

Didrikson angrily insisted that she had known nothing about the advertisement, that the photograph had been used without her permission and the quotation fabricated. She also stated that her car was not a gift—that she had paid for it with her own money. The dealer who placed the advertisement backed up Didrikson's story. He said that she had praised her

car spontaneously, and that he had passed the information on to his superiors without her knowledge. This had become the basis for the controversial advertisement. A letter found in the company's files further proved that Didrikson had not cooperated with or received payment from the Chrysler Corporation, the manufacturer of Dodge cars.

The AAU reinstated Didrikson's amateur standing, but the unpleasant incident forced her to reconsider her future. Realizing that she did not want to spend the rest of her athletic career under the suspicious scrutiny of the AAU, she decided to enter professional athletics. Now she faced a whole new set of challenges, for in the 1930s female athletes had few ways of making money in sports. They could do little more than take up a variety of exhibition and promotional activities, in which they displayed their talents but never engaged in any serious competition. The only legitimate athletic competitions open to women at the time were amateur tournaments that offered no remuneration. Didrikson wanted to play golf, but she knew that she could make no money at it. In order to make a living as an athlete she would have to branch out into other ventures, some of them quite bizarre, many downright demeaning.

Didrikson found her first promotional work with the Chrysler Corporation, which, according to her, felt "sorry about what had happened, and . . . wanted to make it up to me." Appearing at the Detroit Auto Show in December 1932, she signed autographs, played her harmonica, and talked about her car, all in the name of boosting sales of the Dodge coupe. She also hired a manager, George P. Emerson, the man responsible for creating the troublesome Dodge advertisement. While Emerson worked to arrange a series of stage appearances on the RKO vaudeville circuit, the Associated

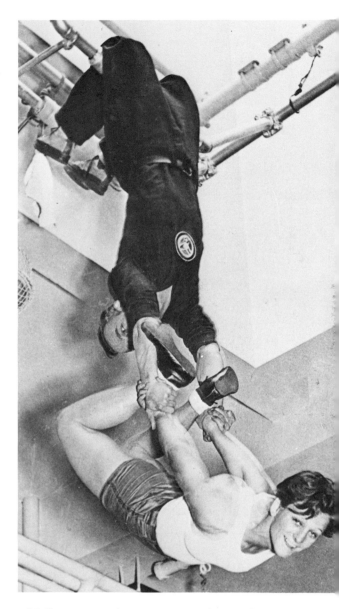

Didrikson practices a gymnastic routine. Although audiences loved her lively shows, the athlete said, "I don't want the money if I have to make it this way."

Press news agency named Didrikson its Woman Athlete of the Year. Her spectacular performance at the 1932 Olympics had earned her a place in history.

Didrikson soon signed a contract with RKO (a major Hollywood production company) to debut at the Palace Theatre in Chicago, where she received top billing over movie actress and singer Fifi D'Orsay. Eighteen minutes long, Didrikson's act opened with a song. After she sang, she put on running shoes and jogged on a treadmill, winning a race against an unidentified competitor. She then jumped a hurdle and drove plastic golf balls into the audience. A reviewer for the Chicago *Tribune* wrote that one of Didrikson's fellow performers "bemoans the fact that the limited scope of the stage forbids her showing more of her extraordinary prowess, such as heaving the discus, flinging the javelin or tossing a basketball."

According to the same critic, Didrikson closed her act by playing her harmonica "with no mean [small] skill." Didrikson's harmonica playing, according to biographers Johnson and Williamson, "was so accomplished that when one listens to her recordings, she sounds as if two or three people were performing together." Chicago audiences loved Didrikson's strange show, which played for a week. Promoters offered her as much as $2,500 a week to continue in vaudeville,

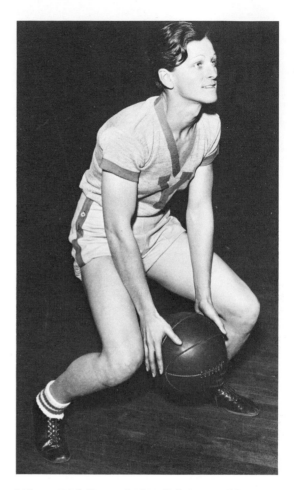

When Didrikson helped the Brooklyn Yankees defeat the Long Island Ducklings, she earned $400 and a live duck, which she sent to her parents in Texas.

but she had grown tired of the theater and wanted to compete again. "It was still in my craw that I wanted to be a champion golfer," she wrote later.

"I don't want the money if I have to make it this way," Didrikson told her sister Esther Nancy. "I want to live my life outdoors. I want to play golf." Although Didrikson disliked the seamy world of exhibition sports, in which she was viewed more as a curiosity than a truly gifted woman, she was determined to make a living as an athlete. She decided to stick with professional sports until she had saved enough money to support herself as an amateur.

For her next engagement, she traveled to New York City, where Emerson had arranged for her to play an exhibition basketball game with a team called the Brooklyn Yankees. The evening that Didrikson played, the Yankees faced the Long Island Ducklings in Brooklyn's Arcadia Hall. Two thousand noisy, excited fans crowded into the auditorium to see the women play. Didrikson was in for a wild evening. "Was that other team ever rough!" she exclaimed. "I never got pushed around and fouled so much in any basketball game. They were determined I wasn't going to make a single basket."

Through all the punching and shoving, Didrikson played grimly on. When she fell and tore her shorts, she refused a time-out and battled on in tatters while the hall rocked with cheers. Her performance recalled the triumphant days with the Golden Cyclones. "On one play I took the ball at center court and dribbled all the way through them to score," she wrote. "I jumped so high and hard going in for the basket that

A skilled pool player, Didrikson nonetheless could not beat billiards great Ruth McGinnis, who had played the game since childhood.

my arm hit the backboard, and I wound up in somebody's lap about six rows back." Didrikson's drive paid off: She scored 9 points, the Yankees won 19–16, and she earned $400 for 40 minutes of work.

Didrikson's next move in her conquest of the big city was a billiards match against Ruth McGinnis, probably the era's best woman pool player. McGinnis crushed the overconfident Didrikson, and the New York press began to criticize the brash Texan. Most sportswriters dismissed her as an immature braggart, but one, Joe Williams of the *World-Telegram*, took advantage of her downfall to attack all female athletes, Didrikson in particular.

Williams belittled the achievements of women champions, comparing them with those of male high school athletes: "The same year [Didrikson] became the greatest woman athlete in history, a comparative chart shows that she had not equalled one record made by a masculine high school champion of the same period." Of course, Williams's criticism was invalid. As Didrikson's biographers Johnson and Williamson put it, "it was like saying that Henry Armstrong or Sugar Ray Robinson were less splendid as boxers because they were too small to defeat heavyweights such as Joe Louis or Rocky Marciano."

Williams further weakened the force of his argument by claiming that women did not belong in athletics at all. "It would be much better if [Didrikson] and her ilk stayed at home, got themselves prettied up, and waited for the phone to ring," he wrote. Unfortu-

In January 1933 Didrikson played exhibition hockey with the New York Rangers, adding to her already lengthy list of sports experiences.

When Didrikson saw golf pro Stan Kertes (kneeling) play in Los Angeles, she said to him, "Gee, you swing nice. Can you teach me that?" For six months, he did.

nately, Williams echoed the sentiments of a whole segment of American society in the 1930s. Although many had found Didrikson, the young Olympic star, an entertaining phenomenon, they felt threatened by Didrikson, the grown woman, demanding to be taken seriously as a professional athlete.

Still, Didrikson would not be discouraged. She returned briefly to Texas, then in March 1933 moved with her sister Lillie, their mother, and $1,800 to California, where she intended to take a few years off and concentrate on learning golf. "I have enough money to last me three years and I intend to win the women's amateur golf championship before those three years and my bankroll are gone," she told a reporter in Los Angeles.

Didrikson's fame brought her into contact with many celebrities. While in Los Angeles, she met Amelia Earhart, the aviator who had made history on May 21, 1932, by becoming the first woman to fly solo across the Atlantic Ocean. Didrikson remarked that Earhart had "the most beautiful hands in the world," and they became fast friends. The athlete greatly admired the courageous flier, who invited her to come along on one of her long-distance flights. Didrikson turned down Earhart's offer, but the two women would remain very close until Earhart's tragic disappearance over the Pacific Ocean in 1937.

Didrikson's $1,800 lasted only 6 months in Los Angeles, but before it ran out she had managed to advance her golf game significantly. She met Stan Kertes, a young golf pro who taught such movie stars as Al Jolson, the Marx Brothers, and Bob Hope. He offered her free lessons and free practice time at the driving range where he worked. Obsessed with learning all she could, Didrikson "used to hit a thousand, fifteen hundred balls every day," said Kertes. "Her hands would blister up and bleed. She wore tape on them all the time. Babe would hit eight or ten hours a day. We'd work until eleven o'clock at night.... I never charged Babe a penny." Didrikson practiced throughout the spring and summer. When their money ran out in September, the three women packed up the Dodge and drove back to Beaumont.

Didrikson went back to work for Employers Casualty at $300 a month, but when her father fell ill she started looking for a way to make more money. She signed up with an Iowa promoter, Roy Doan, to play on a traveling basketball team called Babe Didrikson's All-Americans. In November 1933 the team—four men and three women—piled into one car; for the next five months, they drove from town to town in the rural East and Midwest. They played high school, amateur, and semiprofessional men's teams, winning two out of every three games they played.

As the team's star attraction, Didrikson was paid more than her teammates—and much more than the average working woman during the depression. She made $1,000 per month, while women garment workers, for example, made less than $5 a week. Largely due to Didrikson's presence, the team made a healthy profit

Didrikson kept her distance from her teammates on the House of David baseball team, with whom she had little in common besides an interest in the game.

and the other members were generously compensated as well. Didrikson sent most of her earnings home. One of her teammates recalled that "our manager would pay her in cash from gate receipts. She would go to the bank and convert it into a thousand dollar bill and mail it in an envelope to her folks in Beaumont, Texas. After we explained that this was a careless thing to do, she finally made out a money order."

Didrikson stayed with the All-Americans until the spring of 1934, when she left for Florida. There, she pitched in a few exhibition games with major league baseball teams in spring training. She was generally a controlled pitcher, but not particularly powerful, and the pros had little trouble hitting against her. Nonetheless, she enjoyed herself in Florida, where she met baseball stars Dizzy Dean, Jimmy Foxx, and her hero, Babe Ruth. She received $200 for each inning she pitched.

When the spring-training season ended, Didrikson joined the House of David barnstorming baseball team. Her new teammates, known across the country for their beards, belonged to a small Christian brotherhood based in Benton Harbor, Michigan. That spring a New York *Post* headline blared: FAMOUS WOMAN ATHLETE PITCHES FOR WHISKER TEAM. Somewhat embarrassed by her situation, but unwilling to forgo the ample income, Didrikson kept her distance from her teammates. "I was an extra attraction to help them draw the crowds," she wrote. "I didn't travel with the team.... I had my own car, and I had the schedule, and I'd get to whatever ball park they were playing at in time for the game. I'd pitch the first inning, and then I'd take off and not see them again until the next town."

The House of David played a grueling 200 games over the next few months, winning most of the time. Whenever she had time between games, Didrikson found a driving range and worked on her golf game. It was an intense, exhausting period for her. Her father was still sick, her mother had also become ill, and Didrikson was now the principal breadwinner for her parents. That responsibility, plus the grind of constant travel and dissatisfaction with the course of her career, tempered her naive optimism with a new, studied pragmatism regarding her future.

At the same time, Didrikson was increasingly viewed less as a "wonder girl" than as a sort of sideshow freak. Her detractors attacked her for travel-

Although she later denied it, Didrikson occasionally donned a football uniform and demonstrated surprising skill on the gridiron.

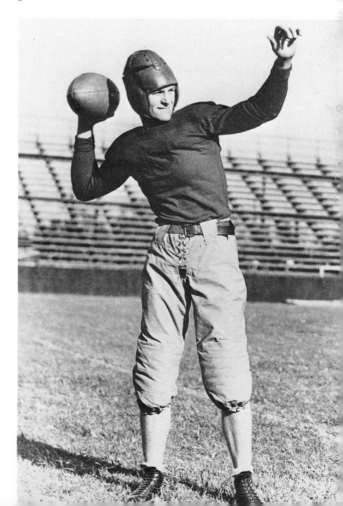

Didrikson's powerful swing helped her score a sensational 77 in the qualifying round of the first golf tournament she entered.

ing around the country "like a vagabond" and competing against men. In Texas, her home state, when women's gymnasiums posted signs with the message "Don't Be a Muscle Moll," everyone knew to whom they referred. For no other reason than that she was a woman, it seemed almost impossible for Didrikson to win the respect and recognition she deserved as one of the era's finest athletes.

Despite her problems, Didrikson was as determined as ever to continue in sports. In September 1934 she resigned from the House of David team and returned to Texas, still thinking about golf. When golf champion Bobby Jones played an exhibition in Houston, Didrikson went to watch him. "I was impressed by the way he stepped up there on the tee and slugged the ball," she recalled. Though rain cut the match short, she never forgot the day she saw the world's greatest golfer play. The experience intensified her ambitions.

Hoping to resume her job at Employers Casualty and to find some support for her golf career, Didrikson spoke directly with Homer Mitchell, the company's president. He put her back on the payroll as one of his secretaries and arranged to pay for her membership at a country club as well as lessons with the club's pro, George Aulbach. Didrikson set about improving her golf game. By November 1934, at the age of 23, she felt confident

To support herself while training to compete in tournament golf, Didrikson returned to work at Employers Casualty, where she was a secretary.

enough to enter her first golf tournament, the Fort Worth Women's Invitational.

Before the first round, Didrikson told reporters, "I think I'll shoot a seventy-seven." She did just that, winning a qualifying medal and causing a sensation in the press. The Texas newspapers trumpeted, WONDER GIRL DEBUTS IN TOURNAMENT GOLF: TURNS IN 77 SCORE. Didrikson was elated to have reestablished herself in legitimate sports, and she loved the publicity—it had been too long since she had received such accolades. Although she was eliminated after the first round of match play, she remained philosophical: She had not expected to win, and she knew that her game was far from perfect, but she had at last taken the first step toward establishing a golf career.

Didrikson now set her sights on the Texas Women's Amateur Championship, scheduled for the spring of 1935. She intended to be there, and she intended to win the tournament.

Although she had to struggle to gain acceptance as a golfer, Didrikson was happy to be playing at last the game she loved best.

FIVE

Teeing Off a New Career

Babe Didrikson decided to shoot for the Texas Women's Amateur Championship Tournament at the urging of two new friends: R. L. and Bertha Bowen. The Bowens, prominent Fort Worth citizens powerful in the Texas golf world, had seen Didrikson play in the Fort Worth Invitational. Impressed by her athletic talent and determination, they befriended her and encouraged her to continue in tournament competition. Didrikson would benefit from their unlikely but genuine friendship for years to come.

In January 1935 Didrikson began practicing fanatically for the championship. She described her daily routine: "I got up at the crack of dawn and practiced from 5:30 until 8:30, when I had to leave for work. I worked until

lunch time, then had a quick sandwich and spent the rest of my lunch hour practicing in the boss's office, which was the only one that had a carpet.... When the lunch hour was over, I went back to work until 3:30. After that I was free to go out on the golf course.... I'd hit balls until my hands were bloody.... After it got too dark to practice any more, I went home and had my dinner. Then I'd go to bed with the golf rule book." On weekends she practiced all day.

Early in April, Didrikson sent her entry form to the the River Oaks Country Club in Houston. Tournament officials received it uneasily. Golf, then largely a country-club sport, was generally played by wealthy society women, a background Didrikson cer-

By the time Didrikson entered her second tournament, sportswriters extolled her golfing skill. One wrote that she "puts the ancient Greek athletes to shame."

tainly could not claim. Some members of the Texas Women's Golf Association complained unofficially about the working-class woman's bid to play golf with them. But when the organizers double-checked Didrikson's Beaumont Country Club membership (country-club membership was the basic requirement for tournament players), they found it valid. Didrikson went to Houston, and in a round on April 22 qualified with a score of 84 strokes.

Golfers generally qualify for tournaments by earning scores that meet a minimum standard set by tournament organizers. At River Oaks, 32 women met the challenge and entered match play. In match play, golfers compete one-on-one, and 18-hole rounds are scored on the basis of the number of holes won by each. The player finishing a hole in the fewest strokes wins the hole and earns one point; the player who wins the most holes wins the round. Play stops when one player leads the other by more points than can be made up in the holes that remain, for instance by three points when only two holes remain to be played. Throughout Didrikson's golf career, most tournaments used the match-play system. Today, most tournaments employ the rules of medal, or stroke, play, in which the player finishing the entire course in the least number of strokes wins the round.

In her first round at River Oaks, Didrikson eliminated her opponent, finishing the round six points ahead with five holes left to play, or "six and five." She won her second round eight points up with six holes to play. Didrikson's unexpected success in one of the country's most prestigious amateur tournaments soon attracted the attention of golf fans and the press. Her gallery, the group of spectators who followed her from hole to hole, grew larger each day. Winning the quarterfinals three and two, Didrikson headed for the semifinals.

In the semifinals Didrikson pulled ahead of her opponent by two points in the first nine holes. Heavy rain halted play for a few hours while everyone waited nervously. When the golfers returned to the course, Didrikson lost her lead. Going into the 18th, the two women were tied. Both players made it to the green in three shots. In *Whatta-Gal,"* biographers Johnson and Williamson describe what happened next: "Winger putted; the ball stopped at the edge of the hole, less than an inch from dropping. She had a five. Babe putted, uphill; she whacked the ball hard. It spurted water all the way up the green, slowed as it approached the cup, seemed to stop at the lip—and dropped in." She had a four.

According to an Associated Press reporter, "Babe smiled, walked off the green—still America's wonder girl athlete and probably the most promising woman golf player in the United States." Didrikson, however, faced a tough opponent in the finals: Peggy Chandler, three-time finalist in and one-time winner of the state championship. Even without her competition, the next day's play—18 holes in the morning, 18 in the afternoon—would be rough enough. But Didrikson loved a challenge.

The morning of April 27 found the course still soggy. Didrikson beat Chandler by 3 strokes on the first hole, and by the 12th hole she led by 5 points. Didrikson seemed unstoppable, but then she faltered. Her drives

To win the Texas Women's Amateur, Didrikson had to beat Peggy Chandler (right), who had won the state championship the previous year.

landed in groves of trees, her putts missed the cup, and Chandler won the next 6 holes to lead by a point after the 18th. Chandler increased her lead to three points by the sixth hole of the second round, and looked like a sure winner. Slowly, however, Didrikson recovered and began winning holes, tying up the match on the 33rd.

On the 34th hole Chandler got to within 2 feet of the cup with 3 shots and seemed sure to take the hole in 4. Didrikson's ball, however, had not even made it to the green after her second shot. It was stuck in a muddy rut, almost entirely submerged; Didrikson would be lucky even to tie with Chandler on the hole. But as she later recalled, "I thought of everything I'd been taught about how to play this kind of shot....I swung, and I did everything right, and I dug that ball up there.... And then there was a roar, and the people behind me came rushing up, and somebody knocked me face down into that muddy ditch. The ball had gone into the hole for an eagle three."

That shot won Didrikson the hole and put her ahead by one point. The two golfers tied the 35th hole, preserving Didrikson's lead. On the last hole, Didrikson finished in three shots, Chandler in five. Didrikson had won the tournament, two points up. Across the nation, sportswriters sang her praises. Didrikson herself wrote: "I was on top of the world that day.... I was

Bertha Bowen (right) and her husband R. L. took a great interest in Didrikson. They used their influence to help advance her golf career.

rolling at last.... now I was ready to shoot for the national championship."

Babe Didrikson, the unrefined 23-year-old from Doucette Avenue, had shaken up the genteel golf world. Her powerful presence on the links threatened to overturn everything "ladies'" golf stood for. Not surprisingly, the United States Golf Association (USGA), the body responsible for governing amateur golf, began to receive complaints about the unconventional new player. Two days after Didrikson won her first championship, the USGA ruled that "for the best interest of the game" Didrikson would be considered a professional. Her past involvement in other professional sports, claimed the organization, disqualified her for amateur golf.

Didrikson called the Bowens for advice. Bertha Bowen later told interviewers how she felt about the USGA decision: "I was just furious at those people who had been so cutting to her. The fact that she was poor and had no clothes did not mean she had to be ruled a professional." The Bowens consulted a lawyer, but to no avail. Then the Beaumont Country Club, which Didrikson had represented in the Texas championship, petitioned the USGA to grant a hearing. The USGA refused. That left Didrikson eligible to play in just one tournament: the Western Open, the only formal competition then open to women professionals.

In response, Bertha Bowen set to work, using her considerable influence in Texas golf to transform the amateur Fort Worth Invitational into the professional Texas Open. Before long, professional women golfers had a second tournament in which to play. The first Texas Open would take place in October 1935. To keep in top competition form until then, Didrikson entered the Western Open. She made it to the quarterfinals but then her playing slipped unaccountably. She lost, but not before hitting a few of her trademark 250-plus-yard drives, including one that traveled an astounding 336 yards.

At the Western Open, Didrikson held a press conference to announce that she had signed a contract with the Wilson Sporting Goods company. She would represent their line of products for $5,000 per year. Teaming up with Gene Sarazen, the first golfer to have won all four of the major men's tournaments, Didrikson set off on a two-month tour, playing exhibition matches in New England, the Midwest, and on the East Coast. In addition to the money she received from Wilson, Didrikson earned $150 for every day she played with Sarazen. "Babe was worth it," said Sarazen. "She had a gift of playing to the gallery. It just came naturally to her. She had the natural ability at golf."

Not only did Didrikson make money on the tour, she learned a lot about golf from Sarazen. "She was very intense and wanted to learn," he recalled. "She'd stand ten feet away from me and watch everything I did. Then she'd go out and practice it for hours." Her driving, always outstanding, got even better; now she routinely hit the ball 300 yards—a distance few men and no other woman golfer could match. Sarazen also taught Didrikson

As a professional promoting Wilson sporting goods, Didrikson toured the country with champion Gene Sarazen, who had much to teach her about golf.

how to deal with such tricky situations as water hazards and sand traps. "After being on an exhibition tour with Gene Sarazen," she remarked, "sand and I were friends."

Didrikson gained valuable experience by playing exhibition matches against some of the best golfers in the world. She took on the incomparable Joyce Wethered, who had won the English Women's Championship five years in a row. At the age of 34, Wethered had already retired from active competition. If Didrikson could beat her, her budding career would receive a tremendous boost. But Didrikson had other things on her mind.

On the night before the match against Wethered, publicity agents from the Goldsmith Company offered Didrikson a huge sum to play with their clubs. Didrikson knew she would probably lose the next day if she used unfamiliar equipment, but, as Sarazen recalled, "She liked the money, Babe did, and she accepted their offer on the spot. My God, we go out the next day and. . . . She couldn't hit the ball at all. . . . Was Babe upset about losing to Joyce? Naw. She said, 'Squire, I got me some do-re-mi,' and she laughed."

Didrikson and Sarazen concluded their tour in time for Didrikson to prepare for the Texas Open. In Fort Worth she confronted a hostile community of country-club golfers who did not want to admit her to their ranks. The atmosphere seemed to undermine her game; she was defeated early on in the tournament. Didrikson relied on her friends R. L. and Bertha Bowen for emotional and social support during the tournament, staying with them at their home. Bertha Bowen said of this period of Didrikson's career, "She used her bravado as a defense, but she really had a rough time in those early days of golf. It's hard to break into society when they don't want you."

Didrikson had difficulty gaining acceptance in the world of golf not only

Didrikson faced Joyce Wethered, five-time British golf champion, in exhibition play. Competing against top players helped Didrikson improve her game.

Didrikson's hard-driving approach to golf forever changed the women's game, which had historically emphasized graceful form rather than strength.

because of her low social and economic status, but because she challenged conventional notions of femininity. Women, current attitudes held, should be weak, soft, and submissive. Aggressively outspoken, visibly muscular, and stronger than most men, Didrikson made many people uncomfortable, particularly those at the pinnacle of society. During her early celebrity, Didrikson frequently referred to feminine fashion as the proper domain of "sissies." She felt that worrying about physical appear-

ance interfered with a woman's ability to pursue meaningful goals. The young Didrikson also resented expectations that she would marry, at one point warning a reporter, "Don't ask me whether or not I'm going to get married. That is the first question women reporters ask. And that is why I hate those darn old women reporters."

Didrikson finally realized, however, that if she wanted to play one game—golf—she would have to play another—conformity. Around the time of the first Texas Open, she let her hair grow out from its short cut. She borrowed some of Bertha Bowen's dresses and makeup, then went out and bought her own. The press commented excitedly about her "transformation," but she said, "I don't believe my personality has changed. I think anyone who knew me when I was a kid will tell you that I'm still the same Babe. It's just that as you get older, you're not as rambunctious as you used to be. You mellow down a little bit."

As if to prove that she was "the same Babe," Didrikson set her sights on competing in the Los Angeles Open, a professional tournament for men. After a few weeks in Texas, she headed for southern California with her parents, her sister Lillie, and her youngest brother, Arthur. The family rented a Los Angeles apartment near the Paramount movie studios, living on the income from Didrikson's contract with the Wilson company.

Didrikson concentrated on polishing her golf game, taking lessons from Stan Kertes, practicing long hours each day, and playing exhibition matches. In the summer of 1937 she went to Illinois for three months to fine-tune her driving form with the help of renowned golf teacher Tommy Armour. With his help, she greatly improved her driving accuracy.

In 1938 Didrikson entered the Los Angeles Open. Although it was historically a men's tournament, no rule explicitly excluded women from competition. Any golfer who scored well enough on the first 36 holes of play qualified to compete in the final 36. Didrikson signed up for the first round and was assigned two partners, both part-time golfers. One was a Presbyterian minister and professor of religion named C. Pardee Erdman. The other was a smiling, husky professional wrestler named George Zaharias.

Babe Didrikson and George Zaharias shared similar backgrounds, interests, and ambitions. They were married 11 months after they met.

SIX

The Golfer and the Wrestler

W hat an introduction George and I had!" wrote Babe Didrikson of the 1938 Los Angeles Open. "One minute we were saying hello, and the next minute photographers were crowding around and calling for him to put wrestling holds on me." After clowning for the cameras, Didrikson and Zaharias teed off for the first round of golf, accompanied by Erdman. By the end of the round the two athletes were joking, "We're getting along so well, Reverend, you may just have to marry us!"

George Zaharias, the oldest son of Greek immigrants, had grown up in a one-room adobe house in Pueblo, Colorado. "I always remember our being in a starved condition," his sister recalled of their desperately poor child-

hood. To help make ends meet, young George started working as soon as he could. He shined shoes, played pool for money, and worked as a roustabout for a traveling circus. Eventually making his way to Chicago in search of opportunity, he responded to an advertisement that read, "Wrestlers Wanted—1 Dollar A Day." Soon he was on his way to fame and fortune.

Six feet tall, weighing 200 pounds, with shoulders so wide he had to turn sideways to go through a doorway, Zaharias made an imposing professional wrestler. His acting skill contributed just as much as his physique to his success in the ring. He skillfully played the role of a villain who fought unfairly and met defeat with tears. Wrestling fans eagerly paid to watch

During the 1930s, when professional wrestling enjoyed tremendous popularity, George Zaharias reached the peak of his fame and became very wealthy.

the "Weeping Greek From Cripple Creek" (a town near Pueblo) get trounced and cry. In his prime, Zaharias made as much as $100,000 a year, sometimes taking home $15,000 for a single night's work. By the time Didrikson met him, he was a wealthy man.

Didrikson and Zaharias took to each other immediately. Perhaps because of that, neither did very well in the first round of the Open. They went out to dinner that night and played the second round together the following day, even though they knew neither of them had a chance of qualifying for the third round. For weeks afterward, they spent almost all their time together. Then

Babe Didrikson married George Zaharias on December 23, 1938. The golfer's husband proved invaluable in managing her skyrocketing career.

Didrikson took Zaharias home to meet her family. "Everything was OK with everyone right from the start," he recalled. "After that, I was always looking for her at driving ranges and she'd leave me notes that said 'Romance was here.'"

Both athletes continued working, Didrikson playing exhibition matches and Zaharias wrestling almost every night. After a few months they got an apartment in St. Louis, where they were married on December 23, 1938. Because of their numerous professional obligations, they did not take their honeymoon until April 1939, when they went to Australia. Zaharias, a shrewd businessman, had arranged a series of wrestling matches and golf exhibitions there.

In her autobiography, Babe Zaharias wrote about the boat trip to Australia: "We were traveling first class, and it was like a morgue. . . . There was no action. . . . So we asked the purser to switch us to a third class cabin. . . . we figured we'd have a better time that way. And we were right. We met a swell gang of people in third class. There was a whole troupe of entertainers going over to perform in Australia."

Babe Zaharias was a hit in Australia. Playing golf exhibitions in most of the nation's major cities, she dazzled the Australian public with her prowess. She also won over the press, who had doubted the stories they had seen in the foreign media. "What this magnificent specimen of athletic womanhood showed us certainly was impressive," wrote one journalist. "The plain fact is that Miss Didrikson is a vastly better golfer than ... any other woman we have seen.... she may get a place among the best men professionals in golf."

When the Zahariases returned to California in the fall of 1939, George Zaharias decided to quit the wrestling ring. At the age of 37 he was already a millionaire, while at 28 Babe Zaharias still had many years of golf ahead of her. The former wrestler devoted himself to managing his wife's burgeoning career, which now changed direction. The couple agreed that the two professional tournaments then in operation did not offer enough opportunity for women to establish themselves as top-flight golfers. Promotions and exhibition play provided a satisfactory income, but not enough challenge or recognition. The only way to reach the top of women's golf, they felt, was as an amateur.

Babe Zaharias needed to get her amateur standing back, and now, married to a wealthy man, she had the means to do it. According to USGA rules, golfers who had played professionally for not more than five years could regain their amateur status by fulfilling two requirements: They needed letters of endorsement from four people prominent in amateur golf, and they had to sit through a three-

year waiting period, during which they could not accept payment for play or commercial endorsements. Zaharias could not have met the second of these conditions before her marriage, for she had relied on the income from professional work. But now she could afford to give it up.

In January 1940, Zaharias applied for reinstatement to the USGA and canceled all her contracts for professional work. She and George Zaharias settled down for the wait in a rented duplex in west Los Angeles, where she gardened and puttered around the house. She kept her game sharp with plenty of practice, and to keep in competitive trim, she entered the two open tournaments—the Western Open, held in Milwaukee that year, and the Texas Open. After stipulating that she would not accept any prize money, she proceeded to surprise everyone by winning both tournaments.

Zaharias's victories made her impatient to play as an amateur. The USGA's regulations had cut down on the competitive golfing she could do while she waited, so she channeled her excess energy into a new game: tennis. She started taking lessons at the Beverly Hills Tennis Club from Eleanor Tennant, who had taught many women tennis champions, including Alice Marble. With characteristic vigor Zaharias pursued perfection in the game, playing as many as 17 sets a day. "There was hardly a day when I didn't

With her boundless joie de vivre, *Babe Didrikson Zaharias had fun and won the affection of golf fans wherever she went.*

wear holes in my socks, and I ran the soles off one pair of tennis shoes after another," she recalled in her autobiography.

Although George Zaharias protested that she was working too hard, Babe Zaharias had made up her mind to compete in the Southwest championships of the U.S. Lawn Tennis Association (USLTA). By the fall of 1941, she felt confident enough to apply for entry to the tournament. Unfortunately, however, the USLTA held that anyone who had at any time played any sport professionally was forever ineligible to compete in amateur tennis. When Zaharias found out that she would never be permitted to participate in amateur competitions, "that took the fun out of tennis for me.... I quit tennis cold."

Restricted in golf, barred from tennis, Zaharias developed an interest in bowling. She took lessons and "put in a lot of long nights at the bowling alleys." Her tremendous strength allowed her to throw "a straight powerhouse ball that thundered down the alley like an express freight train," according to biographers Johnson and Williamson. The versatile athlete also learned the more effective hook shot and started competing in a number of leagues. As in almost every other sport she tried, Zaharias excelled and soon became known as one of the finest amateur women bowlers in southern California.

On December 7th, 1941, the Japanese air force attacked the United States naval base at Pearl Harbor, Hawaii. America was at war, and the country turned its attention and resources to defeating Japan in the Pacific and the Axis powers (Germany and Italy) in Europe. Much organized athletic competition—including many golf tournaments—was suspended. Nonetheless, Zaharias maintained a high profile during the war years, helping sell war bonds by playing in celebrity golf exhibitions. She played with Hollywood stars such as Bing Crosby and Bob Hope, and golf greats such as Ben Hogan and Sam Snead.

In wartime exhibition play, Zaharias specialized in entertaining the gallery with her earthy wisecracks, slapstick antics, and trick golf shots. She would tee up five balls and drive all five of them so fast that the last would be in the air before the first hit the ground. Or else she would stack one ball on top of another and drive the bottom one down the fairway while the top one

Zaharias receives the 1940 Western Women's Open trophy. Because she had renounced her professional status, she could not accept any of the prize money.

hopped into her pocket. Spectators loved her, and she had a great time herself, all the while keeping her game in shape.

On January 21, 1943, the USGA reinstated Babe Zaharias as an amateur. Her first amateur appearance, a 36-hole charity match at the Desert Golf Club in Palm Springs, California, foreshadowed the glorious amateur career that lay ahead of her. She shot an astonishing 70 on the first 18 holes and a breathtaking 67 on the second, smashing the women's record for the course and soundly defeating Clara Callender, the state champion. A week later, she beat Callender again to take the midwinter championship. Over the next year and a half, Zaharias played in a number of charity matches and minor tournaments, but because of the war she did not have the chance to play in a major tournament until the summer of 1944. During this time, her father died of a heart attack.

Zaharias's first major tournament as an amateur was the 1944 Western Women's Open in Indianapolis, Indiana, which she had won as a professional in 1940. She clinched the title again and went home to California, where she spent the next year playing in a variety of matches. In the meantime, George Zaharias had started relocating his wrestling-promotion business from Los Angeles to Denver, Colorado, and Babe Zaharias prepared to move to the Rockies. In the midst of all

Tennis coach Eleanor Tennant helps Zaharias refine her forehand swing. The golfer's natural athleticism allowed her to master the new game quickly.

Flanked by Bing Crosby (left) and Bob Hope, Zaharias watches pro golfer Patty Berg tee off at an exhibition promoting the sale of World War II defense bonds.

this activity, she returned to Indianapolis in June 1945 to defend her title in the Western Women's Open. No one had ever won the Open three times. She intended to be the first.

Babe Zaharias had gotten off to a strong start in the Open, easily winning her first match, when George Zaharias called from Denver. Hannah Didriksen, aging and diabetic, had suffered a heart attack and was in critical condition in a Los Angeles hospital. When the golfer announced that she would fly to California immediately, her husband told her, "Your Momma wants you to finish the tournament." She

played in the quarterfinals the next day and won, then tried but failed to get transportation to Los Angeles. It was wartime, and transportation was hard to find. Military personnel had priority for seats on planes and trains, and gasoline was strictly rationed.

Stranded in Indianapolis, Zaharias played in the semifinals—and won. That evening, her sister Esther Nancy called to say that their mother had died. Distraught, Zaharias promised to return to the West Coast, but her sister urged her to "go ahead and win that tournament. That's the way Momma would want it." Ignoring her sister's

The day following her mother's death, Zaharias managed a smile after defeating Dorothy Germain (left) to win her third Western Women's Open title.

words, Zaharias frantically tried to find a way home—but with no success. On the evening before the finals, unable to leave the Midwest, Zaharias had dinner with some of the other women who had played in the tournament.

Peggy Kirk Bell, one of the golfers, described that night to biographers Johnson and Williamson: "We knew her mother had died and we all expected her to default. . . . Babe just sat there and played her harmonica. She played for hours. She didn't speak, she just kept playing the harmonica." The next day in the morning round, Zaharias set a new women's record for the course with a score of 72. Five points ahead going into the afternoon round, she had to defend her lead against a rally by Dorothy Germain. She did so, and won the match four and two. Zaharias was still the champion.

Early the following morning Zaharias boarded a plane for California. In Kansas City, Missouri, she lost her seat to a high-priority passenger and had to wait for hours before getting a seat on another flight. She made it as far as Albuquerque, New Mexico, before being bumped again, then got on another plane that took her to Phoenix, Arizona. Finally, two days after setting out, she completed the last leg of her trip and arrived in Los Angeles for her mother's funeral, which her brothers and sisters had delayed so she could attend. The family buried Hannah Didriksen on June 26, 1945, Babe Didrikson Zaharias's 34th birthday.

In 1947 the mayor of Denver, Colorado, gives Babe Zaharias the key to the city. The golfer reached the peak of her amateur career in the late 1940s.

SEVEN

Winning Streak

A few months after Hannah Didriksen's death, World War II ended. America entered an economic boom, and organized athletic competition resumed its full prewar schedule. Babe Zaharias entered every major golf tournament that she had the time for. In October 1945, she won the Texas Women's Open for the third straight year. In December, the Associated Press named her the Woman Athlete of the Year, the same award she had won in 1932 after her spectacular Olympic performance. "I got a special charge out of that 1945 award," Zaharias later wrote, "because it had been so many years since I'd had this recognition."

It would not be the last time Zaharias would earn such high praise: She was, in fact, on the brink of the most dazzling period of her golf career. In June 1946 she lost the semifinal match of the Western Women's Amateur, but, as she put it, "that was the last losing I was going to do for a long time." For the rest of the year, Zaharias did not lose a single match. Among the victories she collected in 1946, the National Woman's Amateur was the most prestigious. Coming into the match with a 3-game winning streak behind her, Zaharias played flawless golf all week, destroying her opponent in the finals with a runaway score of 11 points up with 9 holes to play. The Associated Press voted her the 1946 Woman Athlete of the Year.

"As an amateur, Babe dominated women's golf as no one ever has; she was its unbeatable queen," wrote biog-

Combining a forceful long game with a precise short game, Zaharias racked up a record-breaking winning streak of 17 matches.

raphers Johnson and Williamson in *"Whatta-Gal."* By mid-1947 Zaharias had won 15 straight tournaments, a record no golfer—man or woman—had ever approached. (Byron Nelson had held the previous record with 11 wins in a row.) But Zaharias was not yet ready to take a break. She decided to try for her 16th win at a competition officially entitled "The Ladies Amateur Golf Championship Tournament, Under the Management of the Ladies Golf Union"—more commonly known as the British Women's Amateur. No American had ever won this tournament, which was considered the premier women's match in the world.

Zaharias set off alone for Gullane, Scotland, the site of that year's tournament. She sailed to Southampton, England, caught a crowded train for London, and taxied through the streets of the British capital to catch a second train to Edinburgh, Scotland. She made it to the station just in time to catch her train, only to find that all the seats were taken and she would have to stand for most of the 10-hour trip. By the time she arrived in a chauffeur-driven car at her inn in Gullane, she was exhausted.

At the North Berwick Inn, the staff did everything possible to make the golf star comfortable, despite the strict postwar rationing of food and other necessities. When, on her first morning in Scotland, Zaharias joked that she wanted bacon and eggs, fried potatoes, toast, and coffee for breakfast, she was surprised to hear the waiter answer, "Mrs. Zaharias, we've got all that. The manager is keeping some chickens out there just for you. And he went to an American boat and got bacon and ham for your whole stay here."

The Scots were curious about the American woman who had mastered their national game. Each day, as she walked to the course to practice, townspeople greeted her in the street, some even inviting her home for tea. When she practiced, she often found herself the object of friendly scrutiny from the windows of the houses that faced one of the fairways. She enjoyed all the attention, and gradually grew accustomed to the peculiarities of the Scottish course, including its flocks of sheep. "There were sheep wandering all over the place," Zaharias recalled. "The sheep were used to golfers, though. When I came along ... the sheep would just step aside.... they had a fellow in a white coat go along in front of me and clean off the greens where the sheep had been. I believe the average golfer just had to take care of that the best he could."

The Scots grew to love Zaharias, both for her golfing ability and for her straightforward, unpretentious ways. One day she mentioned to reporters

Wearing the warm clothes donated by Scottish fans, Zaharias signs autographs at the British Women's Amateur.

that she had not brought the proper clothing for the wet, windy weather of Gullane, and they printed stories about her problem. Gifts of warm clothing poured into the inn; soon packages filled the lobby. Zaharias chose a jumpsuit and a pair of heavy blue corduroy slacks from the pile, then returned the other donations to the senders or gave them to charity.

During one of her practice rounds, Zaharias took a bad swing and chipped

Although followed by a huge gallery, Zaharias had no problem concentrating at Gullane, Scotland. She became the first American to win the British Women's Amateur.

a bone in her thumb. "I didn't want anybody to think I was trying to build up an advance alibi for myself," she said, "so I just wore a glove over it, and nobody noticed." A few days later, the tournament finally started. Zaharias won her first round but, accustomed to playing before cheering American crowds, she felt uncomfortable with the Scottish gallery's silent, serious demeanor.

Despite her uneasiness, Zaharias won her afternoon match in 16 holes. Then she decided to liven things up by playing the two remaining "by-holes." Performing some of her famous trick shots, she soon had the spectators in an uproar. She stood a match against a teed-up ball, so that when she drove the match went off with a small explosion. On the green, she turned her back to the cup and putted the ball into it from between her legs. The audience loved the show, but the next day a sign appeared on the course: Please Do Not Play The By-holes.

From then on, Zaharias played before large, enthusiastic galleries. Of course, not everyone appreciated her flashiness and horseplay. Johnson and Williamson recorded an incident in which "three elderly ladies in proper tweeds and woolen stockings approached Mrs. A. M. Holm, one of England's finest golfers and a quarter-finalist that year, and declared that they felt Mrs. Zaharias to be boastful, immodest, tasteless, and altogether lacking in refinement. Mrs. Holm retorted coldly, 'You are speaking of the finest woman golfer that has ever been seen here.'" When a competitor rather uncharitably warned Zaharias about a "jinx against American women in this tournament," the golfer replied simply, "I didn't come over here to lose."

As determined and confident as ever, Zaharias cut down one opponent after another. In the semifinals she eliminated Jean Donald, considered the British woman most likely to defeat her. Zaharias then faced British golfer Jacqueline Gordon in the finals, before an unprecedented crowd of more than 5,000. The day dawned fair and warm, and Zaharias put on some of the light clothes she had brought with her from the United States. Because her favorite pair of golf shoes had begun to split from the perpetual dampness, she wore an old pair for the match.

Midway through the first 18-hole round, the weather grew chilly and windy. Zaharias began to shiver, but Gordon seemed unaffected and continued to play well. At the close of the round the score was tied. During the lunch break, Zaharias hurried back to the inn for her cold-weather clothes and her good golf shoes, which she hoped to have repaired in time for the final round. She had to search for the local shoemaker in the crowd at the golf course, but when at last she walked up to the tee for the final

George Zaharias joined the 71 reporters who met the triumphant Babe Zaharias on board the Queen Elizabeth *as it steamed into New York harbor.*

round, she wore the right shoes and her warm clothing.

Zaharias pulled ahead of Gordon by one stroke on the first hole, and maintained her lead for the rest of the afternoon. After the ninth hole, she was five points up. Gordon took the 10th hole, the only one Zaharias was to lose all afternoon. On the 13th, Zaharias went 5 points up, wrapping up the match. She had become the first American to win the British Women's Amateur, adding the 16th—and most glittering—link to her chain of victories.

The spectators cheered for 15 minutes. Zaharias signed autographs and danced her own version of the Highland fling while photographers and

An ecstatic Zaharias accepts her trophy after winning the British championship. Her victory made headlines around the world.

In the wake of her British victory, Zaharias was offered astonishing sums to turn professional. Here, she signs a $300,000 film contract.

reporters crowded around. A writer for the *Manchester Guardian* summed up the tournament with these words: "Surely no woman golfer has accomplished in a championship what Mrs. Zaharias has achieved in this one.... she has lost only four holes in six rounds and.... has combined in a remarkable way immense length with accuracy.... She is a crushing and heart-breaking opponent."

After the tournament, Zaharias spent a few days playing some of the famous Scottish courses. Golf, termed in Great Britain "the royal and ancient game," is said to have originated in 14th-century Scotland. Today, the country abounds with uniquely challenging and beautiful courses, the oldest and best known being St. Andrews. Since 1754, that golf club has set the rules of the game for golfers across the world (except in the United States, which has its own governing body), and been the site of history-making tournaments. When Zaharias played venerable St. Andrews, she wrote, "It was a thrill for me to be there.... It carries so many memories of ... golf immortals. And I thought of all the great matches that had been decided ... and the hearts that had been broken there."

Cheering crowds saw Zaharias off for her trip back to America. When the *Queen Elizabeth* steamed into New York harbor, a boatload of reporters and photographers sailed out to meet her. Babe and George Zaharias stayed in New York City for a few days, celebrating and talking to the press. When they flew back to Denver, they were greeted by a parade that featured floats depicting each of the sports that Zaharias had played during her career. The mayor of Denver, the governor of Colorado, and a crowd of 50,000 turned out to applaud the golfer, who was given the key to the city.

After two weeks of rest, Zaharias entered the Broadmoor Match Play Tournament, held in Colorado Springs

Zaharias's professional activities included publicity stunts, such as this harness race, that showed off her impressive athletic versatility.

in early July. Annihilating her opponent in the finals by a staggering margin of 10 and 9, she brought her record-breaking winning streak to a total of 17 matches. Babe Zaharias was now one of the most famous women in America. She was besieged by publicists, advertisers, and promoters who offered her incredible sums to turn professional. Finally, when a movie company proposed to pay her $300,000 to make 10 short instructional golf films, Zaharias could not resist. The deal ultimately fell through, but by then the golfer had made up her mind to go professional. Heading for New York, she bid good-bye to her amateur career.

In New York, Zaharias struck a deal with sports agent Fred Corcoran, who at the time also served as the director of the Men's Professional Golf Association. Corcoran's other clients included Ted Williams, Stan Musial, and Sam Snead. At a press conference in New York, Corcoran and Zaharias announced the athlete's change of status. Corcoran later described that evening to Zaharias's biographers: "When it came to getting headlines, Babe.... had a fantastic feel for publicity.... A guy asked her what her plans were— where was she going to play? 'Well,' she said, 'I'm going to enter the U.S. Open Championship—for *men*.' I didn't know she was going to say this. I don't think she did when she got up there. There was this stunned silence, mouths dropped, and then the press— en masse—made a dash for the phones."

The next morning, newspapers trumpeted the news of Zaharias's intention to compete for the most prestigious men's golf title in the country. That same day the USGA passed a rule barring women from the men's Open. But Zaharias had plenty of other opportunities available to her. She signed a lifetime contract with the Wilson Sporting Goods company, granting it permission to market a line of Babe Zaharias golf equipment. She published a book of golfing tips. Corcoran booked her into major league baseball stadiums, where, for $500 per night, she demonstrated her golfing skill by hitting shots into the outfield. "I had to stick to demonstrating the short stuff," she wrote. Afterward, she worked out with the home team during batting practice, showing off her notable infielding and pitching abilities. On the mound, she once faced batter Joe DiMaggio of the New York Yankees; in a golf-driving contest, she once took on Ted Williams of the Boston Red Sox.

Zaharias played plenty of golf as well. She went on the road, playing exhibition, charity, and professional matches. "The fees were good, but we probably booked too many of them," Zaharias noted in her autobiography. "One month there were seventeen nights that I was on a plane." The intense schedule took its toll: When

Zaharias pitches against New York Yankee Joe DiMaggio. Her biographers noted that "the crowd loved her in ball parks as much as they did on golf courses."

Zaharias entered the first tournament of her new professional career, in October 1947, she was exhausted. She lost the Texas Women's Open to an unknown amateur named Betty Mims White, ending the longest-running winning streak in the history of golf.

But in her next tournament Zaharias made a powerful comeback, winning with a score of 293 strokes on 72 holes, a world-record low score for women's golf. Undeniably, Zaharias was one of the best—man or woman—ever to play golf. In 1947, the Associated Press con-

93

Bobby Jones and Babe Zaharias play a round. Perhaps the best male golfer of all time, Jones "was a great idol of mine," wrote Zaharias.

firmed this, naming her the Woman Athlete of the Year for the third consecutive time. At the age of 36, Zaharias had carved a permanent place for herself in the world of sports. She made a comfortable living as a professional athlete, earning about $100,000 a year. But in spite of all the recognition and rewards, she was not satisfied.

Little change had come to women's golf since the 1930s, and professionals still had few opportunities for serious tournament play. The top money-maker in 1948, Zaharias took home a total of only $3,400 in prize money. Zaharias confronted the same dilemma she had faced eight years earlier: Women needed more professional golf tournaments and larger cash prizes. It seemed clear to Zaharias, as well as to her husband, her agent, and Patty Berg, another woman pro, that women needed a golf association dedicated to developing the professional tour.

In order to set up tournaments that offered prizes, "we needed money, of course," said Corcoran. Zaharias and her colleagues convinced the president of Wilson Sporting Goods to put up $15,000 in prize money if the association got off the ground. In January 1949 the Zahariases, Fred Corcoran, and Patty Berg met in Miami, Florida, and formed the Ladies Professional Golf Association (LPGA), with Patty Berg as its first president. A new era in women's golf had dawned.

Despite steadily declining health, Babe Didrikson Zaharias continued her golf career with remarkable success during the final eight years of her life.

EIGHT

The Last Round

In the first year of its existence, the LPGA had only 6 members and sponsored just 9 tournaments offering a meager total of $15,000 in prize money. But as its founders had expected, the association grew rapidly. Now that there was a formal governing body working to promote professional women's golf, more and more women players became interested in turning pro. Scores of new members flocked to the LPGA and corporate sponsors contributed thousands of dollars in prize money, so that by 1953 women professionals could compete in more than 20 tournaments and win prizes from a pool totaling $225,000.

Babe Zaharias was the star of the professional circuit. Between 1949 and 1952, she won more tournaments and more prize money than anyone else on the tour. Appropriately, she also served as the LPGA's president after its first year of operation. Her name and participation did more than anything else to lend credibility to the LPGA and professional women's golf as a whole. "Babe changed the game of golf for women—not only by bringing along the LPGA, but by her kind of golf," commented Patty Berg. "She came along with that great power game and .... even changed the swing.... Our sport grew because of Babe, because she had so much flair and color."

Zaharias's "flair and color" may have endeared her to fans and drawn attention to professional women's golf, but it sometimes caused friction between the golf star and her colleagues. When combined with her fierce competitiveness, her confidence often came across as arrogance, as when she burst into a locker room before a match and announced, "Okay, Babe's here! Now who's gonna finish second?" Some of the other women on the tour found her prankishness crude and her extreme frankness indiscreet—even where they would have admired similar behavior in a man. "She added a lot of color to the tour at a time when it was needed," conceded golf pro Betsy Rawls, "but she did not add any dignity to the game."

But Zaharias was simply irrepressible, and most people who knew her loved her dearly. The women who toured with her found her outrageously funny—and fun to be with. Peggy Kirk Bell recalls fondly, "I had a very aristocratic-type aunt and one day Babe was in her living room and she lifted up her leg onto a coffee table and said, 'Hey, Aunt Isabelle, isn't that the best-looking log you ever did see?' My poor aunt just mumbled and looked away.... Life was never dull with Babe. She ... loved living. She loved every minute, more than anyone I've ever known."

At the same time that she was burning up the women's pro tour, Zaharias got involved in a variety of other money-making ventures. Dozens of exhibition games and promotional events made claims on her time, and she worked as a teaching pro at two

As founding members of the Ladies Professional Golf Association (LPGA), Zaharias (left) and Patty Berg (center) devoted themselves to promoting women's golf.

country clubs: first at Grossinger's in New York State, and then, starting in late 1950, at Sky Crest Country Club near Chicago. That year she also earned one of the greatest honors of her career: The Associated Press named her the Outstanding Woman Athlete of the Half Century.

In 1951, Zaharias celebrated her 40th birthday and, with her husband, purchased a country club in Tampa, Florida. The couple moved south to live in a house on the grounds of their property, the Tampa Golf and Country Club. There, Zaharias met 19-year-old Betty Dodd, who would be her constant

The native Texan demonstrates her skill with a lasso. An inveterate cutup, Zaharias constantly clowned for friends, fans, and reporters.

companion for the rest of her life. Dodd, a tall, slender redhead, had started playing professional golf at the age of 13, and had seen Zaharias play in 1947. The two women met through Bertha Bowen, who asked Zaharias to take Dodd under her wing. Bowen said of Dodd, "Betty was from a good family and she had many advantages Babe didn't have. . . . but at times she was so confounded careless about how she looked. She'd dangle a cigarette out of the side of her mouth, stuff her hands in her pockets, and slouch around. It was like entertaining a member of the underworld."

Dodd came to Tampa to stay with the Zahariases, and the two golfers soon developed an intimate friendship. For the rest of Zaharias's golfing career, Dodd traveled with her almost everywhere. Bowen recalled that "they did have such fun together. They spoke the same golf language and they enjoyed the same things. They were downright professional with the mouth organ [harmonica] and the guitar." Zaharias and Dodd frequently played together in tournaments; the younger woman's association with the world-renowned golfer gave her own career a big boost. "I would have walked underground to China for Babe

When they met in 1951, 19-year-old Betty Dodd (left) and 40-year-old Zaharias became friends instantly and were almost inseparable until Zaharias's death.

On the movie set of Pat and Mike, *in which she made a cameo appearance, Zaharias gives actress Katharine Hepburn a few golf pointers.*

in those days," Dodd remarked to interviewers. "She was the most famous person in the world and I was her protégée."

George Zaharias, however, grew intensely resentful of Dodd. For several years, the Zaharias marriage had been deteriorating; Babe Zaharias had become increasingly independent in her career, and by the early 1950s she no

longer relied on her husband's professional guidance. According to Dodd, "George was furious. He knew he was losing control of her." While Babe had been climbing to the pinnacle of her career, George had become mired in personal problems, and his compulsive eating and excessive drinking had turned him into a giant weighing close to 400 pounds. The couple had countless serious fights and spent a great deal of their time apart. They tried to maintain a public image of marital harmony, but according to Johnson and Williamson, "they fooled no one who was ever around them for more than a few hours; it was strictly a public relations act." Still, Babe and George Zaharias never divorced.

Meanwhile, Babe Zaharias's career continued to soar. In the spring of 1952, she played a part in the film *Pat and Mike*, in which Katharine Hepburn starred as a championship golfer and tennis player and Spencer Tracy portrayed her manager, with whom she ultimately falls in love. In the film, Zaharias defeats Hepburn in a golf tournament. Shortly after completing the movie, Zaharias underwent surgery for a hernia in her left thigh. By the end of the summer she was back on the circuit winning tournaments, but late in the year she started losing more and more of her matches.

Zaharias felt perpetually exhausted, but she kept competing anyway. Finally, in April 1953, she decided to see a doctor while visiting her hometown of Beaumont, Texas, to play in the Babe Zaharias Open. She won the match by a one-point margin, then went to her doctor's office for a checkup. While he examined her, she recalled, "I could see his face out of the corner of my eye. All of a sudden he just turned white. He didn't say a word. I guess I'd suspected all along what my trouble was. I said to him, 'I've got cancer, haven't I?' "

The doctor sent Zaharias to a specialist in Fort Worth for tests that confirmed the frightening diagnosis: rectal malignancy. She returned to Beaumont and was admitted to the hospital, where she was to receive a colostomy. On April 17, 1953, surgeons removed Zaharias's tumor and rerouted her shortened intestine to eliminate solid waste through an incision made in the abdominal wall. The operation was a success, but during surgery, the doctors discovered that Zaharias's cancer had begun to spread into her lymph nodes. It was terrible news, for lymphatic cancer is inoperable. No one told Zaharias about it.

Betty Dodd moved into Zaharias's hospital room. Telegrams and letters from around the world poured in, wishing the great athlete a speedy recovery. Within a week Zaharias was eating solid food, and 10 days after surgery she was on her feet. She left the hospital on May 18 and traveled with Dodd to the home of her brother Louis, in Newton, Texas. After Zaharias had spent a few weeks recuperating, she and Dodd paid a brief visit to the Bowens, then returned to Tampa in June.

Just 14 weeks after her operation, Babe Zaharias entered the All American Tournament at the Tam O'Shanter Country Club near Chicago. Zaharias and Dodd were paired for every round of play. Nervous that she might injure herself, Zaharias played cautiously and felt dissatisfied with her performance. In the third round of play, Betty Dodd recalled, "she was missing shots and

Just 14 weeks after her 1953 cancer operation, Zaharias, shown here with her sister Lillie Grimes, returned to the professional golf circuit.

Betty Dodd (left) and Patty Berg watch Zaharias drive the ball. Within a year of undergoing major surgery, Zaharias was winning tournaments again.

fighting like mad. She walked off the green and as we headed for the next hole she sat down on the bench in back of the tee. She . . . put her head in her hands and sobbed and sobbed. It was the first and last time I ever saw Babe break down on the golf course." Her scores in each round were a respectable 82, 85, 78, and 84, but Zaharias finished the tournament in 15th place.

One week after the All American, Zaharias took third place in the World Golf Championship, played on the same course. Then, in February 1954, she won the Serbin Women's Open Tournament. The entire sports world turned its attention to her heroic comeback, and the golfer did not disappoint her fans. Her victories that year included the U.S. Women's Open, which she won by an amazing 12 strokes. In a spectacular recovery from an illness that doctors had said would leave her unable to play championship golf again, Zaharias won five tournaments in 1954. For the sixth time, the Associated Press voted her Outstanding Woman Athlete of the Year.

Zaharias went to the White House that year to meet President Dwight D. Eisenhower and help launch a Cancer

Crusade fund drive. The president, an avid golfer, liked Zaharias immediately. In *This Life I've Led* Zaharias described their introduction: "He said 'How do you do, Mrs. Zaharias.' Then he dropped his head and pretended to whisper. 'I'll see you later, Babe,' he said. 'I want to talk to you about this game of golf.'" The athlete and the president enjoyed a warm friendship until Zaharias's death.

In early 1955, Zaharias continued in tournament play, winning a few titles but weakening steadily. She did some promotional work for the American Cancer Society as well, but as her strength faded, her doctor recommended a vacation. In the spring, Zaharias and Dodd went to the Gulf of Mexico for a fishing trip. The vacation did Zaharias good, until one day she ran into some bad luck. Dodd's car got stuck in some soft sand, so the women borrowed a shovel. "Babe started to dig," Dodd said. "She was like a demon. . . . two old men came out to watch and one said, 'God Damn, I never did see no woman dig like that.'" The next day Zaharias's back was racked with pain.

"Now that I look back," said Dodd, "this was the beginning of the end. The cancer had returned, but it took *months* to find it." Zaharias tried to ignore the pain, entering three more tournaments and winning one of them. Finally she returned to Tampa and "practically collapsed. I was in

Zaharias shared an interest in cancer research with President Dwight Eisenhower. The athlete and the president also spent many hours discussing golf.

bed for several days. I figured some rest was all I needed." But she needed more than rest. Zaharias went back into the hospital, where doctors operated on her back for a ruptured disc.

Neither the operation nor medication relieved Zaharias's intense pain. The doctors, who could detect no physical problem, decided that Zaharias was pretending to be in agony because she was addicted to painkillers. When they confronted her, she became furious and refused further medication in order to prove them wrong. Soon, Betty Dodd recalled, "she was in so much pain that she couldn't eat ... A psychiatrist, Grace Jamison,

Babe Didrikson Zaharias, the feisty Texan who took the sports world by storm, helped pave the way for women seeking careers in athletics.

[was] called in. She talked to Babe and she told the doctors that Babe was not addicted, that she was not imagining the pain, that there was something very physically wrong. . . . Finally they found it, in the lower spine . . . the cancer. There was no way to operate on it."

At the end of July 1955, Zaharias went home to Tampa. With Dodd at her side, she played a little golf and wrote her autobiography. Her health deteriorated slowly for the next several months, and she went in and out of hospitals. When she was admitted to the hospital in Galveston, Texas, in March 1956, she was never to leave again. Zaharias asked Dodd to go back on the tour to keep up her career, and called her sister Lillie Didriksen

Grimes to stay with her. It took months for the cancer to break the athlete's strength, but finally, on September 27, 1956, Babe Didrikson Zaharias died.

Athletes, celebrities, and fans around the world mourned her passing. President Eisenhower expressed his own grief at a press conference, announcing, "Ladies and gentlemen, I should like to take one minute to pay a tribute to Mrs. Zaharias, Babe Didrikson. She was a woman who in her athletic career certainly won the admiration of every person in the United States, all sports people all over the world. I think every one of us feels sad that finally she had to lose this last one of all her battles." Patty Berg remarked, "Thinking about Babe ... I have to smile—with Babe there was never a dull moment. Her tremendous enthusiasm for golf and life was contagious."

Babe Didrikson Zaharias left a legacy of pride, determination, and unsurpassed athletic achievement. In an era when women athletes were viewed as aberrations and had few professional opportunities, she refused to be discouraged. By her example and her performance, she legitimized women's athletics; by founding the LPGA, she opened the door for professional women golfers and set a precedent for the development of other women's sports.

"My goal was to be the greatest athlete that ever lived," she said in her autobiography. She unflaggingly pursued this dream, and in the eyes of many, she fulfilled it. Her excellence in so many sports—basketball, swimming, track-and-field, baseball, tennis, bowling, golf—made her unique as an athlete. This remarkable versatility and almost supernatural talent prompted at least one sportswriter, Grantland Rice, to call Babe Didrikson Zaharias "the greatest athlete of all ... for all time." The legend remains untarnished.

FURTHER READING

"Babe Is Back." *Time* 62 (August 1953): 44.

Gallico, P. "Farewell to the Babe." *Readers Digest* 70 (January 1957): 21–23.

Johnson, William Oscar, and Nancy P. Williamson. *"Whatta-Gal."* Boston: Little, Brown, 1975.

Knudson, R. R. *Babe Didrikson: Athlete of the Century.* New York: Puffin, 1985.

Martin, P. "Babe Didrikson Takes off Her Mask." *Saturday Evening Post* 220 (September 1947): 26–7.

Masin, H. L. "Texas Tomboy." *Scholastic* 50 (March 1947): 25.

Schoor, Gene. *Babe Didrikson.* Garden City, NY: Doubleday, 1978.

"Tell Everybody Hello." *Newsweek* 41 (April 1953): 43.

"Whatta Woman." *Time* 49 (March 1947): 69.

Wind, Herbert Warren. *The Story of American Golf.* New York: Knopf, 1975.

Zaharias, Babe Didrikson. *This Life I've Led.* San Diego: A. S. Barnes & Company, 1955.

Zaharias, George. "Babe and I." *Look* 20 (October 1957): 88.

CHRONOLOGY

June 26, 1911	Born Mildred Ella Didriksen in Port Arthur, Texas
1915	The Didriksen family moves to Beaumont, Texas
1928	Babe Didrikson makes the Beaumont all-city and Texas all-state basketball teams
1930	Joins the Employers Casualty Company's Golden Cyclones and moves to Dallas, Texas
1932	Wins the Amateur Athletic Union national track-and-field championship for the Golden Cyclones in Evanston, Illinois
	Wins two gold medals and one silver medal at the Olympic Games in Los Angeles, California
	Associated Press (AP) names Didrikson Woman Athlete of the Year
1934	Didrikson enters her first golf tournament in Fort Worth, Texas
1935	Wins the Texas Women's Amateur golf championship
	Turns professional after the United States Golfing Association (USGA) revokes her amateur status
1938	Meets George Zaharias at the Los Angeles Open
	Marries George Zaharias
1940	Wins the Western Women's Open for the first time
1943	The USGA reinstates Zaharias as an amateur
1944–45	Zaharias wins the Western Women's Open for the second and third times
1946–47	Achieves a 17-match winning streak
1947	Wins the British Women's Amateur Championship in Gullane, Scotland
	Relinquishes amateur status and turns professional
1949	Founds the Ladies Professional Golf Association (LPGA)
1950	AP names Zaharias Outstanding Woman Athlete of the Half Century
1951	Zaharias meets Betty Dodd
1953	Undergoes surgery for cancer
1954	Wins five major tournaments, including the U.S. Women's Open
	Is named AP Woman Athlete of the Year
Sept. 27, 1956	Babe Didrikson Zaharias dies

INDEX

PICTURE CREDITS

Elizabeth A. Lynn is a writer who lives in Berkeley, California. She holds a bachelor's degree from Case Western Reserve University and an M.A. in English literature from the University of Chicago. She has published one short story collection and six novels, including *Watchtower*, which won the 1980 World Fantasy Award. Her most recent work, *The Silver Horse*, is a children's fantasy book.

❖   ❖   ❖

Matina S. Horner is president of Radcliffe College and associate professor of psychology and social relations at Harvard University. She is best known for her studies of women's motivation, achievement, and personality development. Dr. Horner serves on several national boards and advisory councils, including those of the National Science Foundation, Time Inc., and the Women's Research and Education Institute. She earned her B. A. from Bryn Mawr College and Ph.D. from the University of Michigan, and holds honorary degrees from many colleges and universities, including Mount Holyoke, Smith, Tufts, and the University of Pennsylvania.